How to Get the Job

Learn Solutions from Proven Exemplary Performers

Enhance Your Career Or Start Your Own Business

By

DOUGLAS C MEAD

Seasoned Human Performance Consultant

Copyright © 2013 DOUGLAS C. MEAD & ASSOCIATES INC. 2010
205 Lyon Lake Road
Marshall, Michigan 49068

All rights reserved. No part of this publication may be reproduced, stored in a retrieval system, or transmitted in any form or by any means, electronic, mechanical, photocopying, recording, or otherwise, without the prior written permission of the publisher.

ISBN: 0989717704
ISBN-13: 9780989717700

PURPOSE of this book	To guide an individual or teams in surviving a layoff, downsizing, fulfilling a desire to start a new career, or starting a new business
ACCOMPLISHMENTS/ OUTPUT	• Solutions that produce a new beginning in position/career/business • A custom-designed strategic plan for your future • A custom-designed tactical plan for your future; a step-by-step intelligently designed job-search strategy • Preparations to ensure a successful interview • Scheduled job interviews and a feeling of being part of a team • Confident interaction with interviewers, knowing you have received honest coaching, feedback, reinforcement, and recommendations from your friends, family, and professional relationships • A job leading to a career and/or a business of your own • Income/revenue • A new beginning in position/career/business • A feeling of pride and joy • A feeling of being part of a team and feeling good about yourself • A happy family • A sense of security and pride • Reduced stress • If you create a business, a maximized price paid by the ultimate buyer of your company with the best terms possible

WHO should use this job aid	1. Anyone who is preparing for a new career, laid off of a job and needs a transition plan, anyone who has a desire to start a new career, or anyone who has a desire to start a new business for the first time and is not sure where to begin
2. Anyone who does not have the assistance of a professional job service organization
WHEN to use this job aid	1. After a layoff to bridge the gap between being unemployed and having the new job, a successful career, or a business of your own
2. At the first indication of a layoff
3. If you have not succeeded in letting go of the past and moving on with your life
4. When you are ready to start a new business for the first time
HOW to use this job aid	1. Use this book (job aid) as a tool for learning what to do and what not to do to be successful.
2. Follow the steps as literally as practical, and in the sequence defined.
3. This book (job aid) is designed to be interactive. Use paper and pencil or a computer to take notes for yourself.
4. Document your responses to the questions to create your own personal strategic and tactical plans.

You will increase the probability of producing your personal strategic and tactical plans if you document your responses to the questions and take notes on actions you intend to follow up on, either on paper or on your computer. |

CONTENTS

Section 1: How to Get the Job and/or Start a New Career.................1
   Analysis..1
   Remember 3

Unsuccessful in Getting the Job or Starting a New Business?.........4
   Diagnose the Causes of Your Lack of Success to Date 5
   Potential Root Causes 6
   Understanding Yourself: Identify What You Do Not Need............8
   Recognize the Reality of the Current Situation......................9
   Deal with Your Emotional Change 10
   Deal with Your Logical Change 14
   Deal with Your Physical Change and Your Health 15
   Design a Move-Forward Strategy and Personal Strategic Plan 16

Manage Your Personal Skills, Knowledge, and Information Needs.....24

Design Your Personal Motivation and Incentive Plan 27

Design Your Personal Environment for Success 30

Develop Your Network Team, Your Personal Performance Support System 32

Understand Your Job Market 40

Identify Your Options 45

Redesign and Rebuild Your Career 46

Design Your Tactical Plan. 49

Design and Develop Your Personal Marketing Plan (Including a Top-Quality Résumé) 55

Prepare Thoroughly for Your Job Interviews. 64

Test Your Strategic and Tactical Plans. 76

Implement Your Execution Plan: Nail the Interview 79
    Questions You Should Ask 84

Evaluate Your Performance after Your Interview 88
    Good Practices for Keeping a Job. 89

Section 2: Steps to Start and Sustain Your Own Business 91
    Output that will be produced at the end of this section: 91
    Analysis. 94

Design an Exit Strategy as One Component of Your Business Plan. 101

Perform a Due-Diligence Business Audit. .104

Consider a Franchise Business 108

Design and Develop an Excellence Model for Your Company 110

Develop Your Quality Gap Analysis 112

Design and Develop Your Financial Strategy Plan 113

Design and Develop Your Marketing Strategy Plan 119

Design and Develop Your Management and Organization Plan 121

Design and Develop Your Operation Plan 125

Design and Develop Your Implementation Plan 127

Design and Develop Your Executive Summary...................129

Design and Develop Your Continuous Improvement Plan to
Sustain Your Professional Performance over Time................130

PURPOSE OF THIS BOOK

- Are you preparing to start a new career?

- Are you attempting to return to work after an extended absence?

- Are you underemployed, or are you one of the many people who have stopped looking for a job and are in need of a transition plan for your future?

- Is your support network not working as well as it should to help you accomplish your goals?

If you answered yes to any of these questions, this book is designed to help you produce custom-designed solutions that are explicitly linked to your specific needs and the accomplishment of your business objectives.

This book's message is that **you can** get the job, change your career, or build your own business.

My purpose for writing this book is to share my skills, knowledge, and information resources to help individuals engineer well-thought-out strategic and tactical plans to accomplish their career goals.

How to Get the Job

Being a human-performance business consultant for over thirty years has conditioned me to respond when I know people need help. Given the current economic environment and the need for companies to hire new people, and numerous people's need to get the job, start a new career, or start a new business, I have decided to share the many lessons I have learned while working with companies on over two hundred successful human-performance projects.

Just to be perfectly clear up front, this book is not designed to be an epic novel for your literary enjoyment. This book is also not about the history of acquiring a job, or about great jobs I have acquired over the years. This book does not provide the only approach to accomplishing your goals, nor does this book claim to provide all the answers.

However, this book is designed to help you become a problem solver and a problem preventer. It will teach you how to **reveal solutions** to your specific problem, whether that is getting the job, changing your career, or building your own business.

This book is also designed to

- identify principles to help you produce your own move-forward strategy, personal strategic plan, and tactical plan for success based on your personal and/or business objectives;
- provide you with **a structured process** to guide you through the many phases of the change process;
- help you identify and think through your alternatives and options and then **make the choices that will work best for you**; and
- **help you take the "ready, aim, and fire" strategy to success** instead of the "ready, fire, and aim" strategy that fails to lead you to success.

This book builds on lessons learned in solving problems in the business world. It also builds on the lessons learned from people who are successful in hiring exemplary employees, people who have successfully been hired by companies, and people who have started and grown their own businesses.

This book outlines a problem-solving process for success that I have learned from my own experience, many co-workers, mentors, professional workshops, business books and articles, and people I have interviewed and observed who have successfully used several different forms of problem-solving processes. The problem-solving process within this book has been designed specifically to reveal solutions to meet your needs.

Questions for You

- Have you clearly identified an issue or a specific problem and the root cause of the problem you are faced with at this time?

- Have you or has someone you know given up looking for the next job opportunity?

- Are you or is someone you know tired of rejection, frustrated, or embarrassed for not yet finding the job, or only finding part-time work?

We are quickly moving toward a global solution economy. However, the first step is to clearly define and analyze the problem and define the true root cause of the problem. Only then can you truly identify the most useful and appropriate solutions to any issue. For example, if you have not yet been able to get the job, then why not? What is the true cause of the difficulty? Once you have identified the true cause, then you can determine the best effective solution(s).

How to Get the Job

So what is a solution? A solution is a specific answer to, or way of answering, a problem. If your issue is that you have not been able to get the job or start a new career, or you are not sure how to start a new business, then this book is designed to help you follow a simple and easy process to identify specific answers to improve your situation.

Many people fear change. The reality is that change can be a good thing if you follow several basic principles and a structured process to guide you through the many phases of change and solving difficult issues.

There are more jobs available than you might think. There are approximately 3.7 million jobs available in the United States at the current time. The fact is the majority of jobs available are not posted or advertised publicly. The vast majority of the hiring process is completed by friends and acquaintances hiring other trusted friends and acquaintances. Those jobs go to someone who knows someone, which is why creating a support network is so very important.

While creating a support network is important in finding a job, many people are deciding to take their support networks and become entrepreneurs and start their own new businesses.

By reading this book, answering the questions, and executing the process and steps provided, you will learn quickly and easily the secrets of how to put yourself in a position to get the job or start your own business.

If you are about to create your own business, this book includes a process to identify customer-designed solutions to get you started on the right foot, increase your revenue, lower your costs, reduce your risks, and ultimately improve your productivity and probability of success. You will learn the secrets of exemplary performers who have been where you are right now and have moved on to accomplishing their vision and their purpose in life.

Book Format

In order to help you be successful, this book is formatted based on extensive research and proven instructional methods regarding how people learn.

If	Then
The goal is to learn about something or enjoy a good story	A great deal of narrative is required.
The goal is to learn how to produce something	**Keep it simple.** Learning what output is required, or desired, and knowing and learning the tasks and steps required to produce that output is what is most helpful.

As a result this book is designed as a job aid that includes both cookbook- and decision-making-style formatting. The content of this book also includes a series of research questions that focus on how to achieve your business goals and objectives.

SECTION 1
How to Get the Job and/or Start a New Career

Analysis

Begin by assessing and analyzing your specific situation. Begin with the end in mind. Ask yourself the following questions about the future you desire for yourself and about what you are most suited to succeed in.

1. Are you preparing to start a new career?

2. Are you attempting to return to work after an extended absence?

3. Is your support network stale?

4. Is your professional expertise rusty?

5. Do you or your family and friends wonder whether you're really committed to getting the job or starting a new business?

6. Do you prefer to be an employee?

7. Do you prefer being self-employed?

8. Do you prefer the security of a full-time traditional job and a paycheck, or would you rather own a business?

9. Are you fed up with bad bosses, dysfunctional workplaces, and the false promise of instant riches?

10. Have you been told you are overqualified for available positions?

11. Do you have a desire to start a new career in a new field?

12. Do you want to be in charge of your own life?

13. Do you want to represent a fundamental change in the form, function, and ethic of American work?

14. Do you have the assistance of a professional job service organization?

15. Have you decided you would rather abandon traditional jobs to strike out on your own? Do you want to become an entrepreneur, start your own business, and create jobs rather than work for another organization?

16. Are you tired and dissatisfied with working for someone else? Do you prefer to declare independence and become a free agent, self-employed, or an independent contractor?

17. Do you prefer to work solo; operate from your home, maybe using the Internet as your platform; live by your wits rather than for a large organization; and craft an enterprise that is simultaneously independent and connected to others?

18. Do you want to abandon the job and forge new ways to work?

19. Do you feel you want to become a self-employed knowledge worker, a proprietor of a home-based business, a temp or perma-temp, a freelancer, an independent contractor, or an independent consultant?

20. Do you prefer to depend largely on your own individual efforts and swap steady salary for pay-for-performance agreements that compensate you in commissions, stock options, and bonuses?

If you answered yes to any of the above questions, then this book has been designed for you.

Remember

- Having a good job and/or a career is often about more than just money and resources. A job and a good career is also about purpose; security; feeling good about yourself; and having pride in what you contribute to yourself, your family, and society as a whole.

- Working provides an opportunity to interact with other people, to be a member of a team, to have a reason to get up in the morning, and to grow as you move through life.

- In today's world, business capital means human capital. You are part of that capital investment.

- Whether you work to get the job or start your own business, you are really working to provide a solution to an employer or a customer's problem.

UNSUCCESSFUL IN GETTING THE JOB OR STARTING A NEW BUSINESS?

Prior to implementing a list of solutions, it is imperative that you carefully and accurately analyze and diagnose the problem. Unfortunately, people often try to execute numerous solutions to solving an issue without adequate understanding of the root cause of the difficulty. In a sense, without realizing it, problem solvers have taken the ready-fire-aim approach to planning the next phases of their lives.

Some individuals often try to move forward in their lives without knowing how to create a comprehensive and effective strategic plan to accomplish their goals.

- What is your vision for your future, and how will you know when you have been successful?
- What do you want to produce? What is the end result?
- How will you know if it is produced well?
- Do you want a regular income with benefits?
- Do you want to produce a specific product? Why?

- Do you really want to produce solutions to customers' needs, thereby producing satisfied customers?

- Do you want to provide a service? Does that mean you really want to help customers reduce cost, reduce stress, increase revenue, or just be happier every day?

- Why have you not been successful in accomplishing your vision?

- What have you not produced that you want to produce?

The data you produce from this analysis will help you better identify the most appropriate solutions to achieve your goals. We will examine each of the potential reasons listed and identify how to effectively find a solution to each root cause.

We will also identify how to create a personal strategic plan to accomplish your professional goals and a tactical plan so you will know how to execute your plan.

Diagnose the Causes of Your Lack of Success to Date

Everybody has a different situation in life. One plan does not fit every situation. In order to increase your probability of success, you need to design a plan that meets **your** specific needs. Ask yourself, your family, and close friends if the following potential root causes are applicable to your situation, and document each answer with absolute honesty to narrow down the true causes of your lack of success to date. Once you have narrowed down the true root cause(s), you can identify specific appropriate solutions to your specific problem. You can also produce an effective and efficient personal strategic plan designed to help you accomplish your specific professional goals.

Potential Root Causes

1. **Skills/Knowledge/Information**
   - Do you lack required skills and knowledge to obtain a new position? Have potential employers indicated that you either need to obtain new training and education or that you are overqualified for a position?
   - Do you have clear goals regarding what you want to accomplish?
   - Do you have a strategy to accomplish your goals?
   - Do you have the ability to create a comprehensive and effective strategic plan to accomplish your goals?
   - Do you lack knowledge regarding how to create a dynamic and effective résumé?
   - Do you lack experience in interviewing?
   - Do you lack experience in the field you are focused on pursuing?
   - Do you lack information?
   - Do you lack knowledge regarding the job market or the companies you are seeking employment with?
   - Do you lack knowledge regarding the process required to get the job or start a new business and what sequence of events is most effective?
   - Do you lack knowledge and experience regarding how to start a new business of your own?
   - Do you lack required training, certifications, and/or degrees to be successful?
   - Do you lack access to simple and useful work instructions?

2. **Motivation and Incentive (Attitude)**
   - This is often a long journey. Are you being continuously focused, patient, and steadfast?
   - Are you demonstrating perseverance?
   - Are your priorities clear?

Unsuccessful in Getting the Job or Starting a New Business?

- Do you receive positive consequences like feedback from a support network for the time and energy you invest in your job search?
- Are you looking for and accepting fair compensation in any job offers to date?
- Do organizations you have interviewed with appear to have fair policies?
- Does your job search involve organizations that appear to have jobs that involve what you consider worthy tasks?
- Are you looking for a job that offers some novelty?
- Do you have sufficient confidence in yourself and your skills, and do you present your confidence in job interviews?
- Are you afraid of success or failure?
- Are you truly interested in working?
- Are you tired of looking for a job?
- Are you insecure?
- Do you really believe you should be working?
- Do you have the motivation and incentive (attitude) to succeed in getting the job or starting a new business?
- Are afraid of the unknown?
- Do you believe you will be successful?
- Do you believe you will fit into a new job?
- Do you have what it takes to perform new required tasks?
- If you are receiving unemployment, do you feel you can find a job that pays more than you are receiving in unemployment?
    - Do you believe that is a useful perspective for long-term success?
    - Is that really the best way to view a tough situation?

3. **Your Environment**
    - Are there no obvious jobs available in your community?
    - Do you think you have you exhausted every possible opportunity where you currently live?

- Are you limiting your options because of your current location?
- Is there a lack of a useful support network team to assist you in your job search?
- Is there a lack of sufficient time available for your job search?
- Have you chosen to make the time available to pursue your job search?

4. **Capability**
    - Are you certified but not qualified for a position?
    - Are you qualified but not certified for a position?
    - Are you overqualified for the positions you are seeking at this time?
    - Are you trying to find a job you may not be capable of performing?
    - Do you meet sufficient requirements for the job?

The remainder of this book efficiently identifies solutions to effectively deal with the causes you have identified for your situation. Read each step carefully and follow the recommendations of people who have been successful in getting the new job, starting a new career, or establishing a new business of their own.

If you combine your true understanding of your real business needs and your current technical and professional expertise, and interpret the information and data contained within this book, the end result will be a new set of targeted solutions that you design for your situation. These new solutions will add real value to you for the rest of your life.

Understanding Yourself: Identify What You Do Not Need

1. List those things and/or people that you **do not** need or want to have in your life any longer, those things or people that you are tired of, or those things or people that are currently making your life unhappy and creating negative energy in your life.

2. You need to learn from the past and then let go of the past.

3. Let go of your former job and how things used to be.
   - For many people, their jobs are their lives.
   - What is done is done, and dwelling on the past is not going to help you plan your future.

4. For you to succeed in accomplishing your goals, you need to eliminate those things that are taking up your time in a negative way (e.g., people, habits, and an unhealthy environment).

Recognize the Reality of the Current Situation

Let's face it: changing jobs, changing careers, or starting a new business can be intimidating. You are used to working with certain people, working within certain work processes, and working within a certain rhythm every day.

> **Note: Change in your life could be the best thing that ever happened to you.**

1. Focus on how to effectively and efficiently develop a plan to not only survive but to thrive and succeed.

2. You need to consider your alternatives and make well-informed critical decisions.

3. You increase your confidence by demonstrating your competence.

Change is inevitable. However, change is and should be a process. Change can be dealt with from at least three process perspectives.

1. Emotional change

How to Get the Job

2. Logical change
3. Physical change

Deal with Your Emotional Change

OK, so you have lost your job. Often the first initial impact is to your personal motivation because you are devastated. For some of you, the first instinct is to be very afraid, feel very hurt, and panic. Your confidence is rocked to the core.

1. You need to get through four predictable phases of change as quickly as you can. The four phases of the change process are sometimes referred to as the SARA syndrome.

    - ✓ Phase 1 is Shock.
    - ✓ Phase 2 is Anger.
    - ✓ Phase 3 is Resistance.
    - ✓ Phase 4 is Acceptance.

2. You need to recognize that different people get through the four phases at different times and at different paces. Some go through all four very quickly and some take longer. There is no right or wrong pace.
3. It is important for you to recognize that once you get through these four phases, it is time to move on.
4. The best and most productive way to deal with these perspectives is to start to develop your own personal strategic improvement plan to comprehensively improve your life.
5. **Do not** be your own worst enemy!

6. **Do not** choose to immerse yourself in negative energy! In fact, you need to immerse yourself in positive energy.

7. **Do not** choose to feel sorry for yourself and dwell on how unfair it is that you have lost your job!

8. Recognize that life is seldom fair, and move on. You need to accept that fact and identify your choices and make decisions that will have a positive impact on your life.

9. You need to choose to develop a positive attitude to be successful. This might sound easier said than done, but it is essential because employers do not need or want employees with negative attitudes.

> **Caution:** Many people make the mistake of thinking a job interview is all about them and what they need or want.

10. Adopt a job-finding attitude.
    - Recognize that there is a significant difference between making phone calls and going to interviews thinking, "I'm looking for a job," versus thinking, "I'm here to do the work you need to have done."
    - When you're looking to get a job, you're expecting someone to give something to you, and you are giving something to them.
    - You still need to focus not only on impressing them but also on making sure you want this particular job.
    - It is very important to make a good impression, but it's even more important to demonstrate your desire and ability to help your prospective employer be successful and achieve his or her business goals.

11. **Do not** focus on and communicate to a potential employer what you need, but instead communicate and focus on how you can help the employer

accomplish his or her business goals. The employer needs to believe you can assist in accomplishing his or her business plan.

12. Everything you write and say should be preceded silently by the statement "This is how I can help your business succeed."

13. You can achieve success if you consistently focus your energy on the most appropriate influences affecting change, which include motivation, incentive, environment, skills, knowledge, information, and capability.

14. To maintain and improve your personal positive attitude, it is important to develop a plan to maintain or improve your mental, physical, and emotional health and increase your personal motivation and incentive to accomplish your goals.

15. To perform at an optimum level, you need to feel good about yourself through physical and mental exercise and by following a healthy diet.

16. There is a strong connection between mental, emotional, and physical health, and all three are extremely important to the achievement of your goals. All three will help you maintain and strengthen your confidence to succeed.

17. Especially when going through a difficult change, focusing on improving and/or maintaining your physical health will not only keep you in good physical condition but will also keep you in good mental and emotional condition.

18. Exercise will provide you with an enormous amount of mental strength and confidence. Exercise will help you think more clearly.

19. Set health goals and be consistent in your workouts.

20. Eating the proper foods and taking the appropriate vitamins will also provide the energy and the sound mind you need to accomplish your career goals.

21. Good nutrition and exercise will increase your personal motivation and incentive to accomplish your goals and produce positive energy.

22. Take some time to mourn the death of the last phase of your life and then move on.

23. Get through these four phases of change as quickly as possible and then get on with your life.

Deal with Your Logical Change

In addition to dealing with your emotional change, you must create and sustain a focus and plan for the future. There are only so many hours in each day to accomplish your goals, and you must use your time productively.

1. Develop a rhythm for each day by planning and scheduling how you will use your time.

2. Set your alarm and get dressed for your new job responsibilities, which are the steps involved with getting the job or starting your own business.

3. Visualize your time available like a picture of a pie. The pie never gets any bigger.

4. Decide how you want to schedule each hour of each day, in a way that will ultimately make you happy.

5. Use a piece of paper and a pencil or your personal computer and identify and document those things that you really need to have in your life for now.

    ✓ Examples: people and a support network, training in writing a résumé and networking skills, and information

Unsuccessful in Getting the Job or Starting a New Business?

Deal with Your Physical Change and Your Health

Physical change deals with your physical health, your appearance, and how you present yourself to others.

1. Pay attention to your personal presentation.

2. Focus on how you look and feel when you present yourself during volunteer work and job interviews.

3. Make sure you dress appropriately when volunteering, networking, and interviewing.

4. Get an adequate amount of sleep each night

> **Note: It takes energy to make the energy you need to accomplish your goals.**

5. Stretch first thing each morning.
   - Stretching for ten minutes every morning has a variety of benefits, including decreasing risk of heart attack, alleviating stress, and improving circulation.

6. Exercise to get in or maintain your healthy physical shape.
   - Your physical health impacts your mental and emotional health.
   - Your physical health also makes you look like someone an employer will want to hire.
   - Replace couch time with thirty minutes of exercise every day.

7. Eat a nutritious diet every day and take vitamins as appropriate.
   - Begin by eating a healthy breakfast every day. When you skip breakfast, your body gets confused and thinks there's a famine. This decreases your metabolic rate and makes it harder to burn calories

throughout the day. A good breakfast that includes fiber helps you eat fewer empty snacking calories throughout the day.
- Eat at the right times each day because it helps ensure you have enough energy and that you have the ability to concentrate.
- Minimize sugar and salt intake.
- Carry healthy snacks like carrot sticks.
- Practice portion control.
    - Take a few bites and then wash them down with a big glass of water.
    - Get the taste out of your mouth or else that drive to have more will continue.

8. To increase your ability to focus on what it takes to accomplish your goals, get at least eight hours of sleep each night.
    - Have a regular nighttime routine to help ensure adequate sleep.
    - If you can't fall asleep in fifteen or twenty minutes, sit up and meditate and focus on your breathing.
    - You will increase the probability of falling asleep right afterward.

9. Reduce stress by showing up early.
    - Being five minutes late is a small thing that creates big stress, which in turn can cause chronic inflammation and high blood pressure.

Design a Move-Forward Strategy and Personal Strategic Plan

Strategy: A plan, method, or series of maneuvers for obtaining a specific goal or result.

Strategic Plan: A broadly defined plan aimed at creating a desired future. The opposite of a plan is often chaos.

A strategic plan will help you step back and think about what you really want to accomplish from this point forward. A good strategic plan can help you avoid the ready-fire-aim approach to securing a job and beginning a new career. By following the steps and answering the questions provided in this book, you will be able to better plan for both your short- and long-term career.

Tactical Plan: A systematic determination and scheduling of the immediate or short-term activities required in achieving the objectives of strategic planning.

Once you have created a well-thought-out strategic plan, the tactical plan will help you identify more specifically what you need to do to accomplish your personal strategic plan.

Whether you're looking for your very first job, switching careers, or re-entering the job market after an extended absence, finding a job requires four main tasks.

1. **Identify and understand what you really want to accomplish.**
2. **Understand yourself.**
3. **Understand the job market.**
4. **Understand what you need to do.**

Find a way to provide yourself useful feedback, hold yourself accountable, and encourage your own success. The focus is on you and how you will create a plan to accomplish your goals. Take a look at where you are right now and then consider where you want to be in the future.

Identify and understand what you really want to accomplish.

1. Clarify and **document** your needs, wants, and short-term and long-term SMART (specific, measurable, attainable, and timely) goals.

- It is time to examine what you need and want to accomplish with the rest of your life. What is your vision and your dream for the future?

Develop a Strategic Plan

1. Write a vision statement. A vision statement is a statement (typically two to three sentences) that describes a mental picture of what an individual or an organization hopes to become or what the person or organization hopes to achieve.
    a. It is important to understand where you are going before you develop a strategic plan on how to get there.
    b. The value of a vision statement is that it gives you a focus for your goals.
    c. Close your eyes and describe the mental picture you see when you have accomplished your vision, mission, and goals.
        i. **Document** thoughts that describe the picture.
        ii. Take some time to play with the wording until it describes your thoughts accurately.
        iii. Example vision statement: "Serendipity will be the premier retail store in Marshall, Michigan, by providing unmatched customer service that meets or exceeds customer expectations."
2. Write a mission statement. A mission statement is an explanation of why you or your organization exists and the path that needs to be taken to achieve your vision.
    a. Mission statements answer this question: **what is your purpose**?
    b. Mission statements are typically shorter than vision statements, but not always. They are individually specific. This is a statement that describes what you are passionate about.

Unsuccessful in Getting the Job or Starting a New Business?

    c. Look at your vision statement and begin to brainstorm a mission statement.

    d. Describe your thoughts and document your answers.
- Example mission statement: "We exist to help our customers select and purchase the most appropriate gifts possible."

3. Perform a strengths, weaknesses, opportunities, and threats (SWOT) analysis.
   - Strengths: Characteristics that may give you an advantage over others.
   - Weaknesses: Characteristics that may be a disadvantage as related to others.
   - Opportunities: Conditions that could potentially increase the probability of accomplishing your goals.
   - Threats: Conditions that could create problems in implementing your plan.

> **Note:** A SWOT analysis is a great exercise to go through because it identifies the key areas that may need targeted resources, as well as opportunities or opposing factors that could affect your strategy. The SWOT analysis process can flesh out many great ideas to help target development, growth, and improvements.

4. Perform a gap analysis.
   - A gap analysis is a process you need to go through to identify the gaps between your current state and your vision.
   - A gap analysis answers the question, "Where are you currently, compared to where you want to be in the future?"
   - The process draws insight from your vision and mission statements.
   - To do a gap analysis, simply look at where you are and compare it to where you hope to be.

- As an example, gaps for an organization could include the following:
    - Market share
    - Financial data
    - Internal process/systems
    - Public relations
    - Critical success factors, which may include customer satisfaction and quality of products/services
- Example of an organization's current state that needs to be improved.
    - Customer Satisfaction scores of seventy-five percent
    - Profit margin of 1 percent
    - Market share of 10 percent
    - Return on poor-quality products is 10 percent
- Think about the rest of your life and determine those things that you want to accomplish within your lifetime. For example, one of my goals is to learn to sail. Another is to continue to help others as much as I can.

5. Create personal and/or organizational goals.
    - Once SWOT and gap analyses are done, it is time to start writing goals.
    - Write SMART goals for two to three years out.
    - Goals are only as effective as the formalized process of achieving them. Many people use the SMART (specific, measurable, attainable, realistic, timely) goal process to ensure their goals are achievable.
    - Produce a description of your SMART goals with the following criteria:
        - **Specific**: Is the goal specific enough for clarity?
        - **Measurable**: Is there a way to measure the success of the goal?
        - **Attainable**: Is the goal truly attainable?
        - **Realistic**: Is the goal realistically written?
        - **Timely**: Is there a timeline associated to the goal to ensure a completion date?

Unsuccessful in Getting the Job or Starting a New Business?

6. As part of the goal development process, include a discussion with your support network members and answer the following seven questions to help facilitate a discussion and thought process that fleshes out the details needed for writing effective goals:

    ➢ Why, who, what, when, where, how, and how well?

7. Once you have answered these questions, create a **goal-setting worksheet** as an easy visual of the goal plan.

8. To ensure useful focus, **begin with the end in mind.** In other words, if you were on your deathbed, what would you wish you had accomplished and produced during your lifetime? Make a list of your wishes, desires, and needs, and then work backward.

9. If you want to get the new job, start a new career, or establish a new business, the first step in the process is to **identify what you really want and need to accomplish**. For example, maybe you want to produce as output

    ✓ a plan to accomplish a new beginning,
    ✓ a job to get you by until you are in a position to advance your career (always remember that it is easier to get a job if you have a job),
    ✓ a good-paying job doing something you know how to do and are good at,
    ✓ a new job or career, and
    ✓ a new successful business of your own.

10. If you don't yet know specifically what you want to accomplish, continue to seek more advice and gather more information.

11. Think about, identify, and document what brings you joy, what brings you a sense of purpose, and what makes you happy and fulfilled.

- Think about, identify, and document what you are passionate about.
- Explore and document your interests, the things that provide fulfillment, and your professional passions.

12. Determine whether you want to stay in your current field but contribute more than you are currently.

13. Use the answers to these thoughts as input to the creation of your personal strategic and tactical plans.

14. To help you grow in your career, visit a career counselor at a local college or a certified career coach, or ask advice from the people in your church or job corps agency.
    - Most community colleges and adult-education centers provide counseling services or classes for adult students who are looking to change careers.
    - Some career counselors will have you fill out worksheets designed to gauge your skills, values, and interests, and assess your personality and your preferences.
    - Some advisors will help you determine the type of work that would be most rewarding and best aligned with your talents and temperament.
    - Before selecting a career counselor, ask for references from clients and find out if they have worked with people in situations similar to yours.
    - Have at least one session with the coach or counselor to gauge your comfort level before you agree to a fee for their services.
    - Do not confuse a coach or counselor with a recruiter who focuses on placement.

15. Find others in your network who have been in similar situations and have been successful in accomplishing their goals.
    - Talk to your spouse or significant other.
    - Talk to your friends and mentors.

16. Visit your local library, where the reference desk librarian has many useful resources.

17. Examine the possibility of working with a job-search organization. Some placement services have the employer pay for the fees.

MANAGE YOUR PERSONAL SKILLS, KNOWLEDGE, AND INFORMATION NEEDS

One important component of professional success is recognizing what skills, knowledge, and information will be required by a potential employer.

1. Identify and document what skills, knowledge, and information you need to meet your potential employer's needs and to accomplish your goals.
2. Fit the job to the skills rather than the other way around. Many people search for jobs, then try to see how they can "tweak" the way they present their own skills and experiences to fit the job description.
3. Instead, document a list of all of your current skills and knowledge.
4. Then retune your skills. Start by documenting a list of work-related skills and knowledge **you need to learn and become proficient in** as you move forward in executing your strategic and tactical plan.
5. Find someone who can help you evaluate your current skills and identify the gaps between your current skills and the desired level of proficiency.

Manage Your Personal Skills, Knowledge, and Information Needs

6. Seek out training that has the following:
    a. **Relevant** training content
    b. **Relevant** practice
    c. **Sufficient** practice
    d. **Timely** delivery

7. Find a coach who can help you reach the desired level of proficiency.

8. Find relevant books and upcoming conferences that would significantly improve your abilities.

9. Your potential employer will be interested in hearing about how you intend to become an exemplary employee.

10. Think about and document which skills and knowledge will make you more competent in the position you're applying for. For example, public speaking, project management, leading a team, and abilities in computer programs are often beneficial.

11. Practice new skills you need like typing, word processing, and navigating in the Windows environment to prepare for the next job opportunity.

12. Because you are sometimes more employable if you have a degree or certificate and some work experience, and because to some employers experience is often more important than education, get experience any way you can.
    - If you are in school currently, don't come out of school with a résumé that only has an "education" section.
    - Get a job while you go to school.
    - Volunteer to gain experience.

13. Improve the effectiveness of your job-search communication skills.
    - Learn how to write job-search letters, how to network, and how to dress for success.

How to Get the Job

- Pay particular attention to presentation, including your grooming and clothing attire.

14. Learn telephone self-marketing techniques and strategies.

15. Learn how to realistically assess and respond to job offers.

16. Learn how to effectively negotiate job offers.

DESIGN YOUR PERSONAL MOTIVATION AND INCENTIVE PLAN

There is a very wise old saying that if you think you can, you will. If you think you can't, you won't. Your career is your responsibility. You own it. Even though you don't know where your career is going at this time, everything you do is building toward a point where you'll turn around and see a career that you can define.

1. Stay true to your character, your beliefs, and your revival.

2. Have enough confidence in yourself as a human being to overcome failure. It may take another week, a month, or more.

3. Competence and confidence are a catch-22. One breeds the other. The more competent you become at preparing for your future, the more confidence you will be able to demonstrate to yourself, interviewers, and decision makers.

4. You **must** develop the confidence that you will succeed.

5. Tell people who you are through your conversations, phone calls, e-mails, and work.

How to Get the Job

6. Work harder and better than everyone around you, then eventually you will rise to the top.

7. Don't forget what it is like to have a sense of purpose.

8. Stay humble.

9. In order to achieve what you want to accomplish, you cannot do it alone. You need to surround yourself with talented people who believe in you. Nurture them, guide them, and then everyone moves forward together.

10. If you continue to push hard, you will not only succeed, you will excel at everything you want to do.

11. Continue to work hard, and you will accomplish your goals.

12. People seek to get the job for different reasons. Determine why you need a job. Identify and focus on **the purpose** of a job for you. Is it
    a. because you desire independence,
    b. because you need to support your family,
    c. because someone told you that you need a job,
    d. to pay the your bills and save and invest for your future, or
    e. because you need to feel you have a purpose in your life?

13. Seek a balance in your life between happiness and professional success.

14. Practice and demonstrate tenacity and perseverance.

15. To truly be successful, you must become **focused** and **passionate** about what you want and need to accomplish.

16. Seek and accept help along the way.

17. **Do not** shut people out who want to help you.

Design Your Personal Motivation and Incentive Plan

18. Spend time with the people who want to help you and with activities that make you happy, bring you joy, and help you accomplish your personal and professional goals.

19. Focus on what you are going to do next.
    - Focus on your vision and dream and keep dreaming of whatever you want to accomplish.
    - Focus your energy on finding your next job, your career, and what work will make you happy.

20. Do something you are passionate about. Chase your vision. Build toward something that will make a difference in your life.

21. Monitor and document your progress every day. Determine if you are making progress toward your goals.

22. Choose to succeed and don't ever, ever, ever give up. If you think about giving up, ask yourself, "What is the alternative?"

23. Your job search is your new job for now. Wake up early every day to get started on your search for the job.

DESIGN YOUR PERSONAL ENVIRONMENT FOR SUCCESS

Many things in your environment can impact your ability to succeed.

Remember, when considering a career path, it is easier to get a job if you have a job. Many employers will consider you more seriously if they know you already have a job and you are working hard to get the job in your chosen career path.

1. Engineer your work environment and ensure you are receiving the correct input to accomplish your goals.
   - Make a plan and a schedule for what you want to produce every day.
   - Check for opportunities every day through whatever sources you are using (newspaper, Internet, friends, family, etc.).
   - Make sure you have access to helpful **work instruction guides** like this book.
   - Make sure you have the proper tools and equipment (computer, printer, etc.).
2. Do you have adequate time to find the best job? Finding a job is now your job. Invest at least eight hours every day.

3. Do you have achievable performance criteria to measure your progress in finding the best job? For example, include in your goals that you will get a job by a specific date, even if it is a part-time job for now.

4. Do you have a manageable workload to find the best job? Do you have competing priorities? Is there any priority more important for you than getting the job or starting your own business?

5. Do you have good work design to find the best job? See how to design strategic and tactical plans later in this book.

6. Do you have job assistance in finding the best job? For example, get a support network.
   - Look for good coaching from people you respect and who have demonstrated success.

7. Do you have adequate conditions? For example, if the problem for you is that there are no jobs available in your community and you have exhausted every possible opportunity where you live, have you considered moving to a new location that does have job opportunities?
   - This action may be very difficult, but is it impossible?
   - Many people have had to take this action and have been successful in getting the job.

8. Is the space where you live and work organized, neat, and clean?
   - Your space will impact your self-image and how you feel about your environment.

9. Are you surrounding yourself with positive influences?
   - If not, then you need to find a way to make that happen.
   - Negative energy will suck the life and the positive energy right out of you.

How to Get the Job

10. Create your personal financial plan.
    - Create a realistic budget, so you can plan for and frequently monitor your required **income** and **necessary expenses**. Part of your environment that impacts your motivation and incentive is knowing how much income you need to meet your basic financial requirements, and how much you can spend on expenses each month.
    - Establish **a baseline** by determining the total of your normal monthly expenses.
    - If there is an imbalance between income and expenses, then you need to establish a creative strategy to find a balance. The worst thing you can do right now is create a bad credit history.
    - A creative strategy could mean the following:
        - Doing things you do not want to do
        - Reducing monthly expenses
        - Finding a way to increase monthly income
            - Maybe finding part-time work
            - Maybe taking someone in to help pay the monthly house payment or the rent

Maybe moving in with family or friends until you do get the job or start a new business

Develop Your Network Team, Your Personal Performance Support System

The expected accomplishment/output that will be produced as a result of developing a Personal Performance Support System:

- A scheduled interview and a feeling of being part of a team

- Confident interaction with interviewers, knowing you have received honest coaching, feedback, reinforcement, and recommendations from your friends, family, and professional relationships

Everything revolves around relationships, how you can help others, and how they can help you. Networking is one of the most effective means of getting the job. Often the best companies to work for rely heavily on employee referrals.

Networking is a targeted strategic method of job hunting. It is popular with organizations that rely on employees to bring in new talent. It is typically cheaper to recruit this way as opposed to placing job ads or searching through recruitment firms.

Very Important

- **There are more job positions available than you may think. The majority of jobs are not posted or advertised publicly.**
- **The vast majority of the hiring process is completed by friends and acquaintances hiring other trusted friends and acquaintances.**

When numerous people are applying for jobs, it is very difficult for you to get noticed.

The key is how well you interact with the people recommending you, those interviewing you, and those who make the decision to hire you.

Knowing this critical fact should help you realize that creating your support-system team and networking can help you receive coaching, practice interviewing, make future decisions as you gather additional information, and identify options available to you.

Personal connections are critically important during economic hard times. You need to interact very well under pressure, solicit referrals, and muster up all the emotional strength and support you can to get through this sometimes-difficult transition time.

It is critical for you to realize that the people and places you involve in your networking process become essential to any direction you take at this stage in your change recovery.

You may be shocked by the long list of people that you know who will welcome the opportunity to help you through these very difficult times.

Some people do not ask for help, either because they are not comfortable, or they feel very independent. For those people I ask, "How is that working out for you so far?"

What many people don't always consider is how many friends and family they have that find **meaning, purpose, and usefulness in helping others**. They will often welcome the opportunity to help you be successful.

1. Create a committed team to help you be successful.
    a. Document a list of all your friends, relatives, and acquaintances.
    b. Network aggressively.
        - Work smarter, not just harder.
        - Create a business card with your contact information, to make it easy for your network and potential employers to contact you.
        - **Do not** confuse activity with productivity.
        - Be disciplined and committed to meeting and talking to potential employers, and take some chances.
        - Look for connections in companies or with people you want to work with.

- Establish a profile on the website LinkedIn.
    - Use the site to obtain information on the types of people a company hires, the name of the hiring manager for a certain job, maybe an e-mail address, and maybe even a personal connection at an organization you are interested in.
    - Use the people-search function on LinkedIn to connect with people you know.
    - Try to find the hiring manager for the organization you are interested in.
    - Put your LinkedIn public profile hyperlink in your automatic e-mail signature. This is an elegant way to attach your résumé to every correspondence you send.
    - Even family and friends who think they know you may click through to your profile, learn more about you, and perhaps think of you for a job or lead that they might have overlooked.
- Once you have connected with a contact online, take the conversation to e-mail or a phone call, or schedule a time to meet face-to-face.
- Make cold-call visits in person and hustle for opportunities.
- Use your knowledge of organizations you are interested in to create **customized** cover letters that focus on what you can contribute to a company if you are hired.

2. Begin with people you now know socially and with people you have worked with before.

3. Obtain e-mail addresses, home addresses, and phone numbers.

4. Call each one of your friends, relatives, and acquaintances, and ask them if they know of any openings that they could recommend you for.

5. Request an introduction to a contact at a potential employer organization.
6. Ask if you can use their names as a door opener to get a conversation going with the person or people who make the hiring decisions.
   a. Let them know you do not expect them to do the hard work for you or to necessarily endorse you or even intervene on your behalf.
   b. Don't surprise your friends, relatives, and acquaintances as you move forward. Keep them informed, especially if you plan to use their names as references.
7. Ask for ideas.
8. Ask them to point you to others in your field.
9. Don't be bashful or worried about being forward.
10. Be transparent by initiating open discussions of why you have stopped working. This demonstrates confidence, honesty, and resolve.
11. Be clear in your discussions about why you've taken a break from work.
12. Be straightforward on your résumé.
13. **Do not** try to cover the gaps or skim over these details in conversations. This behavior will make employers suspicious and make you look evasive.
14. Mention your occupational aspirations to anyone and everyone you know and meet.

> **Caution**
> - Don't drive people crazy by obsessing every time you communicate with them, or you will alienate your network.
> - Don't be too humble or apologetic.

Design Your Personal Environment for Success

15. Tell them what you've been looking for, but let them know you're flexible and if they have any suggestions, you're open to them.

16. Make numerous new contacts each month by making cold calls and sending e-mails.

17. Search websites like Indeed.com and Simplyhired.com.

> **Note:** Always remember that it is easier to get a job if you have a job. This is not the time to be picky about jobs; a connection can often get your foot in the door, and you can negotiate pay or switch positions later once you've gained experience and established your reputation.

18. Occasionally touch base with all of your references.
    - The purpose of this is twofold. You can ask your references for leads, and you'll also be refreshing their memory of you in their mind.
    - Hopefully their memory of you is a good one, or else you shouldn't be putting them down as a reference.
    - If a potential employer calls them, they won't hesitate as much when remembering who you are.

19. Find and join a support group.

20. Research volunteer opportunities.

21. Start volunteering for an organization that focuses on something that you're passionate about, or is related to your professional field of interest.
    - You may end up doing boring or easy work in the beginning, but as you stick around and demonstrate your commitment, you'll be given more responsibilities.
    - Not only will you be helping others, but you will also be gaining references and feeling good about being productive.

22. Emphasize your volunteer experience on your résumé.
    - Select one or more volunteer situations that can provide you with opportunities to help make you feel good about your contributions and provide you with connections and contacts that will make you productive.

23. Follow through. Get up early every morning just like you are going to a paying job, and help others every day.

24. Broadly define your network.
    - You don't realize how many contacts you have.
    - Talk to close friends.
    - Consider former classmates, colleagues from earlier employers, business relationships outside your institution, and civic acquaintances.

25. Make it a goal to have quality in-person meetings every week and additional contacts by phone or e-mail.

26. Create a new network along the way. Ask people who else to call. Imagine people you don't know who are relevant to your search. Cold-call them.

27. View discussions as learning opportunities, not just job inquiries.

28. Ask about more than jobs. Ask about the industry, how to succeed, and how to position yourself.

29. Approach these meetings as conversations to break the ice.
    - It's disarming.
    - What you learn may lead you to shift your target or change the way you present yourself.

30. Contact people in different ways.
    - Contact your close professional friends in whatever way is most comfortable.

Design Your Personal Environment for Success

- For more distant acquaintances, and certainly for people you're trying to meet, send an e-mail or a letter followed up with a phone call and then a meeting.
- Buy coffee or lunch. After a substantive discussion, send a thank-you e-mail or letter.
- As further follow-up, go back to people with an update on what you're learning, and ask additional questions.

31. Periodically evaluate your progress and whether to change the approach.
    - View this as conducting a study.
    - Review your notes from different meetings.
    - Look for patterns.
    - Are there better ways to move in the direction you've selected?
    - Are there valid reasons to shift your direction?

32. Ask friends and contacts if there are any vacancies at their company or at their friends' companies.

33. Be systematic with good record keeping. Keep an Excel spreadsheet that includes the following:
    - Name
    - Location
    - Industry
    - Prior career
    - Intensity of relationship
    - Was it an e-mail or a face-to-face meeting?
    - After each interview meeting, write down what you learned and what you'll do as a result.

34. Each week, contact at least twenty-five people and score the quality of each contact from one to ten.

UNDERSTAND YOUR JOB MARKET

To increase the probability of success, it is critical to do your homework to help you truly understand and analyze the market that you are seeking to enter.

1. Analyze and collect market intelligence, and understand the job market.
    - Whether you are a first time job hunter or re-entering the workforce after being laid off or from any type of absence, it is important to look at the employment environment in your area.
2. Document a list of informed and as-accurate-as-possible assumptions. Examples include the following:
    - The product you are selling is you, your experience, and your core competency.
    - Competition for jobs is increasing as management seeks and hires only people who have the most potential for helping boost their organizations' profits.
    - Are there or are there not jobs available in your general vicinity?
    - Do you or do you not have the credentials you need to secure a job in your intended market?
    - Do you or do you not have a network support system in place to help you acquire a job or start a new business?

Understand Your Job Market

- **The people who market their talents best will win.**
- When looking for a job currently, you will be greeted with a job market that is weaker than it has been in years.
- Hiring is expected to be up compared with the levels of the past several years.
- Given the large employee-base transition that is likely to occur over the next five to ten years, there will be an increase in the number of employers looking for recruits at career fairs and on campus.
    - According to projections from the Bureau of Labor Statistics, the labor force in the next ten years will be affected by the aging of the baby-boomers, those born between 1946 and 1964.
    - The annual growth rate of the fifty-five-and-older group is projected to be 4.1 percent, four times the rate of growth of the overall labor force.
- There is a looming **knowledge worker skills shortage** that impacts competitiveness and economic and social development.
- Two factors are fueling the increase in job openings.
    1. Company growth
    2. A wave of retirements that are expected to occur in the coming decade
- Skilled baby boomers are retiring in unprecedented numbers.
- The newly created knowledge-economy jobs require more education and higher skill levels.
- Faced with stiffer competition and tougher hiring requirements, organizations are becoming more focused on productivity and bottom-line performance.
- Human capital jobs sometimes are temporary in the new economy.

3. Are you drawn to a specific industry? If so, determine what industry you prefer.

How to Get the Job

4. Are there job openings in the industry in which you have experience?

5. As you more forward, determine which of the following you want:
    a. The same job in the same industry
    b. The same job in a different industry
    c. A different job in the same industry
    d. A different job in a different industry
    e. Still not sure at this time

6. Identify your core competency.

7. Determine which kinds of businesses and industries need your skill, knowledge, and experience the most.

8. Identify who the major players are in that industry.

9. Find out what they are doing and where they hang out, and insert yourself into their network.

10. Once inside their network, start fishing for intelligence.
    - Who's got staffing issues?
    - Who needs work done that you can do?
    - Who just got a big injection of money into their organization or business?
    - Find that person inside the company that can be your champion.
    - Pick someone in middle management with problems that need solving that you can help with. Research via LinkedIn, pipl.com, and jigsaw.com for managers at companies you'd like to work for; surf their voice-mail systems at night to see if you can get their name, title, and phone extension.
    - Determine how you can best blow them away with the amount you know about them and what they do.

Understand Your Job Market

11. Which industries are growing, which ones are stable, and which industries are in decline?

12. What occupations are in demand? What are typical wages for different jobs?

13. What other conditions may influence the work available?

14. Ask around for advice and find businesses that will benefit from having you and your skills around.

15. It's important that the nature of the job fits your personality and salary requirements; otherwise, you'll have spent a significant amount of time to find a day job you dread getting up for every morning.

16. Think outside the box.
    - Seventy-five percent of jobs are never advertised.
    - Access job opportunities through word of mouth, cold calling, and submitting unsolicited job applications.
    - Be in the right place at the right time.
    - Make sure you have the requirements for the job.

17. Research the company.
    - Don't just do an Internet search; memorize their mission and their business goals.
    - If it's a retail company, visit a few of their stores, observe the customers, and even strike up a few conversations.
    - Talk to existing employees.
    - Ask them what it's like working there, how long the position has been open, and what you can do to increase your chances of getting it.

18. Become familiar with the history of the company.
    - Who started it?

- Where did it start?
- Who runs it now?

19. Be creative, and do whatever you think the other candidates don't have the guts to do.

20. Look for job market information.
    - Numerous resources are available through the Internet that make it relatively easy to keep current with job market trends.
        - The US Bureau of Labor Statistics at www.findtherightjob.com
        - Overseas jobs at overseasjobs.com
        - overseas.indeed.com
        - Local Jobs (Now Hiring)
        - job.com
        - jobsearch.job.com
        - No Experience Needed Jobs
        - www.JobsOnline.net
        - ExpatCareers.com
        - NPRjobs.com
        - #PubJobs Twitter feed

21. Analyze the information you collected and documented.
    - Ask yourself these questions:
        1. What is the good news for me in this information?
        2. What is the bad news for me?
        3. What new ideas does this information give me about jobs I may not have considered before?

IDENTIFY YOUR OPTIONS

We all have choices available and decisions to make. However, often the realistic options are sometimes limited. For example, you may:

- want to find a new job and start a new business on the side,
- want to look for a new job with your former employer or look for a new job with a new employer,
- decide to change careers or go back to school, or
- decide to start a new business.
    1. Each career path is unique. Examine all your options so you can make an informed decision. The decision on what you want to accomplish will determine your tactical strategies regarding how to accomplish your goals. For example, an option might be the military. Joining could lead to a good career in the military even after the civilian job market improves.
    2. Collect information and seek advice and recommendations from your significant other, friends, colleagues, and other people you respect.
    3. **Do not** let not accomplishing your goals be an option. **Do not** choose to fail.

REDESIGN AND REBUILD YOUR CAREER

Stop and think carefully about what you really want and need to accomplish with your career. The following list represents actions and questions that are designed to help you analyze what career is best for you.

1. Prioritize your list of expected employment accomplishments and goals. **Establishing your priorities** is probably the most important action you can take. On a scale of one to ten, which accomplishments and goals are most important to you?

2. Why are they important to you?

3. Write down today's date and then the date you expect to accomplish each of your future goals. The date provides a benchmark for measurement of progress. This date not only serves to provide a new focus in your life, but also serves as criteria that you can evaluate your progress against achievement of your goals.

4. Further clarify your own personal expectations.
    - Review your goals for the following criteria:
        - Time you expect it to take to accomplish each goal
        - Quality of your résumé, as well as appearance and accuracy of spelling and grammar
        - Quality of your interviewing skills

Redesign and Rebuild Your Career

- Resources required
- Sequence
- Is there logic regarding the order in which your goals need to be accomplished? For example, obtain financing before purchasing office equipment.
- Develop a flow-chart diagram of your goals and identify the input and output of each goal.

5. If you want to transition to a new job, create a "fresh ideas" list.
   - Keep a list of ideas for your future–hobbies you enjoy, your areas of expertise, business ideas you passed on previously, childhood dreams, and every pipe dream you've ever had.
   - Narrow the list down to what interests you most, what you can make happen, and what you want to learn more about.
   - Try out different fields by volunteering, taking classes, and talking to those who have the position you want.
   - Rather than starting off on your own, take advantage of jobs that have been newly created or for which demand is growing.
   - More employers are reporting that within their organizations, new jobs are emerging that didn't exist five years ago. These include positions tied to the following:
     - Cybersecurity
     - Green energy and the environment
     - Storing and managing data
     - Financial regulation
   - Organizations are hiring in large numbers in some areas, including those that affect revenue and innovation. If you're looking to get some new experience before launching an independent career, here are some areas where employers are hiring first:
     - Customer service
     - Information technology

How to Get the Job

- Sales
- Administrative support
- Business development
- Accounting/finance
- Marketing

DESIGN YOUR TACTICAL PLAN

If your vision and goals include looking for a new job, then create a job-search plan.

1. Create a step-by-step intelligently designed tactical job-search strategy.

2. Develop an action plan.
   - Identify the specific tasks and steps required to accomplish each goal.
   - Flow-chart the tasks in the sequence they need to be performed.
   - Identify resources required.
   - Identify potential problems.

3. Manage your job search in the most efficient and effective manner possible.

4. Do not be shy about asking for work and telling someone why they should hire you, even if you don't already have a job.

5. Decide your next career steps and what you want to do.

6. Select a career direction or a specific job objective.
   - When you know what job or career path you are looking for, you know what information to use in your résumé and what to leave out.
   - This may be easy if you really know what you want to do from now on.

- This task can be difficult if you are not be sure of what you want to do for the rest of your working life.
    - ✓ Determine if you are currently looking for a **specific job** or **a career direction.**
    - ✓ Determine how you want to use your technical and/or mechanical abilities.
    - ✓ Determine your specific area of interest.
        - ✓ Are you drawn to a specific job? Is there a subject, an activity, or an interest that over time has appealed to you?

7. Identify a list of your greatest job-related strengths and skills.
    - ✓ List all of your past job titles. Start with your most recent and work backward.
    - ✓ List all the skills by job title.
    - ✓ List three to five of what you consider to be your greatest skills, and skills you enjoy performing.

8. Go to your local library. There are several books regarding preparing for a job search.

9. Gather information about the company or organization you will be providing with a résumé.

10. Create a résumé strategy. For example, should you pinpoint your best prospects and look for a job in any industry with two or three résumés instead of sending out numerous scattered résumés?

11. If your career goal is to work in public media, go to @NPRjobs and #PubJobs Twitter feeds to help learn about jobs that are available at NPR and to view job-search resources.

12. If you are one of the numerous people who continue to get rejected because potential employers believe you are overqualified based on your résumé, then consider a résumé that focuses on your skills and what you can produce for the organization.

13. Mention that a formal résumé is available upon request.

14. Don't be too picky about which job you get at this time.

15. Find something that you can excel at. If you are cleaning out a barn, learn to be the best barn cleaner there is.

16. If you're working in the trades, move around the organization and learn to do numerous jobs, even administrative roles if possible.

17. All of this will provide revenue, build your résumé, and teach you things about working that you're going to have to learn the hard way no matter what job you have. Examples include the following:
    - How to demonstrate initiative
    - How to effectively deal with interpersonal dynamics
    - How to effectively deal with work politics
    - How to be a good employee
    - How to be a good boss
    - How to be a team player

> **Note:**
> - **Remember, contract and temporary positions often lead to full-time positions.**
> - **Take your experience and shape it into the job/career that you want.**
> - **The things you do earlier in your career will take your future career in new and wonderful directions.**

How to Get the Job

18. To create your own career, do everything required to forge your own path.

19. It may even lead you to self-employment.

20. Consider cold-calling on potential opportunities.

    - If there is a company that you have read about but available positions are never advertised, it may be the time to make a cold phone call and try to get the job.
        - This approach requires confidence, so breathe slowly and deeply and go for it.

> **Note: Personal assistants, technical assistants, and secretaries are trained to screen calls like yours.**

    - Treat them with respect, and they often will be willing to help you.
    - Be polite and courteous, but **do not** appear to be sucking up.
    - Speak to them clearly and with confidence.

21. Say something like, "Hi…my name is…I am calling about advice regarding potential opportunities within your department. Is this a good time to speak to you?"

Design Your Tactical Plan

If	Then
The answer is yes	1. Lock down a meeting day and time. 2. Bring your résumé. 3. If relevant, provide examples of your work.
The answer is "This is not a good time"	1. Act confident and request a better day and time. 2. Request their direct extension and call back at the scheduled time. 3. Keep the discussion brief, focused, and filled with the following: • Your name • Why you are calling • What you want from them (that is, a job, a meeting to discuss vacancies, etc.) 4. Indicate that you would love to have the opportunity to meet them and discuss any possible vacancies that may suit your qualifications and extensive experience. 5. If the answer is no, then ask if you can send your résumé or e-mail your contact details in case something arises in the future. 6. When sending the e-mail, mention that you will send an occasional update via e-mail. This follow-up will help ensure you are remembered and therefore considered when a new position does arise. 7. Make sure your e-mails are concise and not too frequent.

How to Get the Job

21. Keep a record of all the calls you have made and their responses.
    - If they say, "There's nothing now, but call us back in six months," then make a note in your schedule calendar to ensure you follow up.

DESIGN AND DEVELOP YOUR PERSONAL MARKETING PLAN (INCLUDING A TOP-QUALITY RÉSUMÉ)

1. Look for examples of exemplary résumés.
   - Your résumé is your sales brochure and often provides your potential employers with a first impression of you.
   - A well-designed résumé emphasizes your preparation, experience, skills, and qualifications for the job you seek.
2. Design your résumé to survive the thirty-second scan.
   - Your résumé is one of your most powerful sales tools.
   - Your résumé may be one in a thousand or more, so it must be designed to stand out from all the others.
3. Design your résumé to illustrate what you can contribute and what you really have to offer.
   - Be sure you design your résumé in a way that makes you very proud of the design and what you have to contribute to your next employer.
4. Determine the best format for your résumé.

- ✓ A chronological résumé format presents your work history and accomplishments in a strict chronological sequence beginning with your most recent job. You do not identify your skills; the reader decides what your skills are based on your job history.
- ✓ A functional résumé format first identifies your major functional skills, then presents your work accomplishments that illustrate your skills.
- ✓ Create an online showcase of your work. While résumés are static, an online portfolio can demonstrate your purpose and meaning. Include a link to your LinkedIn page and your blog.

If	Then
You are continuing the same occupation and/or industry. Your career shows growth and progressive responsibilities. You have an unbroken employment record with no gaps.	Use a chronological format. 1. Name/Address/Phone 2. Career Summary 3. Accomplishments 4. Career History 5. Education/Profession 6. Military Service 7. Personal/Interest/Achievements
You are making a significant career/job change (e.g., welder to supervisor). You have been employed by the same company for a very long time. You want advancement (e.g., first-line supervisor to manager).	Use a functional format. 1. Name/Address/Phone 2. Career Summary 3. Skills/Accomplishments 4. Career History 1. Education/Profession 2. Military Service 3. Personal/Interest/Achievements

- ✓ Design and edit criteria for your résumé.

Design and Develop Your Personal Marketing Plan (Including a Top-Quality Résumé)

5. Include **useful and factual content** that supports your job or career objective.

6. Present a **classy appearance** using quality white, ivory, or gray paper. Present it in a nice, quality cover.

7. Use a proper **format and structure**. The best résumés are succinct and usually one or two pages long. They always include wide margins, bold headings, and indentions or bullets to guide the reader's eye to the most important parts of the document.

8. Provide a **demonstration of confidence and poise.** Focus on the reader's perception and not your intention. Design for what the reader needs to know about you. Focus on the following:
   a. Proper spelling and grammar
   b. Using active voice
   c. Using consistent tense
   d. Putting statements in positive form
   e. Using definite, specific, concrete language
   f. Cleanliness, accuracy, honesty, and brevity
   g. Not using fancy words
   h. Not overstating your image, knowledge, or skills

✓ Begin by creating a summary.
   ✓ Articulate your job or career objective. This information lets employers know your goals.
   ✓ Design an overview summary of your work history career profile.
      - Offer a view of where you have come from and how that led you to where you are today. It needs to be a clear summary of your work experience that demonstrates why you are qualified for the job you have applied for today.

- If you have been working for many years, all that is needed is information reflecting the last ten to fifteen years of your work history.
✓ If you have been out of work for a while, show a prospective employer that you stayed productive by taking classes or volunteering.
✓ Establish a **personal value proposition** (PVP). It is at the heart of your career strategy. It's the foundation for everything in a job search and career progression, targeting potential employers, attracting the help of others, and explaining why you're the one to pick. It's why they should hire you and not someone else.
    o Set a clear target audience for your résumé, one that needs what you have to offer. Targeting will make you most effective.
    o Identify your strengths: what you know, what you can do, and what you can produce.
    o Tie your most important strengths to your target position. Don't leave it up to the employer to figure out how your strengths relate to what they need. Let your PVP tightly connect you to the position. Consider the perspective of the person hiring and know why they should hire you.
    o Provide evidence and success stories. Your strengths may be what an employer is "buying," but your achievements are the evidence you have those strengths. They make your case convincing. Some people prepare a nonconfidential portfolio to showcase that evidence in a vivid way.
    o Pull together facts on measurable accomplishments such as sales growth or cost reduction.
✓ List any awards or accomplishments in the top third of your résumé.
✓ Answer the question "What can you do for me?" right off the bat with a summary list of the strongest and most relevant accomplishments at the top of the résumé.

Design and Develop Your Personal Marketing Plan (Including a Top-Quality Résumé)

- A list of job accomplishments helps the person or persons responsible for hiring decisions recognize your value and contributions.
- Accomplishmen\ts can be very powerful selling tools because employers are looking for people who can demonstrate they can achieve results.

✓ List what you have produced in your past work. Think "output."

✓ List problems you have solved, goals you have accomplished, and formal recognition you have received.

✓ Remember, "in God we trust and everyone else must bring honest data." So emphasize past achievements by identifying data like performance-measurement indicators, numbers, percentages, and places. Data numbers are powerful selling tools because they demonstrate the magnitude of your achievements. The résumé that articulates a reduction of 15 percent in waste is much more impressive than the one that merely indicates a reduction in waste. Let your accomplishments speak for themselves.

✓ Begin each accomplishment with action words or phrases. Examples include the following:
  - Increased sales by 25 percent in one year.
  - Exceeded performance goals by 30 percent by identifying and solving barriers to improvement.
  - Trained fifty new employees that met performance expectations.
  - Produced seventy-five widgets under budget and ahead of schedule.

✓ List your strengths—the concrete skills and knowledge you've acquired through work experience and education.

✓ Ask others for input without pulling punches. They may mention strengths you don't recognize, raise questions about the strengths you do mention, or ask questions that lead you to imagine new strengths.

How to Get the Job

- ✓ Get the ball rolling by asking questions like these:
  - ✓ What do you think I am best at? What strengths might I build on? What are my weaknesses?
  - ✓ What jobs should I avoid?
  - ✓ What jobs should I target?
- ✓ Revisit past job performance feedback.
- ✓ Research your old performance appraisals and coaching input from supervisors.
- ✓ Think about hiring yourself for your current job.
- ✓ Ask yourself why you would or would not be hired for this job.
- ✓ Revisit your strength list.
  - Return to your first list of strengths and modify it to reflect what else you have learned.
  - Categorize and rank that list.
  - Be specific.
- ✓ List your education and training. Educational background is described briefly, beginning with your highest degree, then major area of study, name of school or college, and date of degree(s) earned.
- ✓ Add additional training or certification if it applies to the job you are applying for.
- ✓ List company-sponsored training if it applies to your job or career path objective.
- ✓ If you do not have a degree, show the highest educational institution attended and subject-sponsored courses, correspondence programs, certificate training, and workshops and seminars that support your job or career path objective.
- ✓ List your most relevant skills; emphasize skills relating to your job objective. Include the following skills if you truly possess them.
- ✓ If you don't presently possess these skills, then do whatever you need to do to acquire them.

1. **Getting along with others**
   - Interpersonal skills are very important because the working environment consists of various kinds of personalities and people with different backgrounds. It is essential to possess the skills of interacting with others and communicating and working with people from different walks of life.
2. **Communication skills**
   - Employers tend to value and hire people who are able to express their thoughts efficiently through verbal and written communication.
   - People who land a good job easily are usually those who are adept in speaking and writing.
3. **Research skills**
   - You should possess the ability to systematically find relevant information through research in order to do effective searches for the data needed by a particular activity.
4. **Logical thinking**
   - Most businesses regard this as the ability to handle and organize information to produce effective solutions.
   - It is the ability to find sensible solutions regarding a spending proposal or an internal activity.
5. **Information technology**
   - Most job openings will require people who are IT or computer literate to know how to operate different machines and office equipment, whether the equipment is a PC or a multifunction copier and scanner.
   - It is critical that you know the basic principles of using technology.

6. **Efficiency and organizational skills**
   - Organization is extremely important to maintaining a harmonious working relationship in the company.
   - Most employers want people who know how to arrange their work through methods that maintain orderliness in the workplace.
7. **Career Advancement**
   - Career advancement is the ability to create a plan that will generate maximum personal and career growth.
   - Be willing to improve yourself professionally by learning new skills to keep up with developments in the workplace.

✓ Make your value known quickly.
   - Most employers give each résumé about a three-second window of time before they decide to either "delete" or read further.

✓ List your personal characteristics (these can be bulleted statements alone or combined with two or three sentences).

✓ List relevant personal interests/affiliations/memberships; these components are optional.

✓ Include things such as memberships, language skills, special achievements, and military experiences if they support your job or career path objective.

✓ If you are in management, show affiliations and/or memberships in professional organizations to your field and profession.

✓ If you are active in your community, include these activities. Be selective and avoid mention of religious or political activities.

✓ List referrals. Either provide names and contact information, or mention they are available upon request.
   - Always give references that you have prescreened to increase the probability of a positive referral. Make sure that your references are predominately managers. An occasional colleague is OK, but

Design and Develop Your Personal Marketing Plan (Including a Top-Quality Résumé)

contemporaries, friends, and family members really don't carry much weight in helping you land a position.
- Once you create a powerful résumé, it will be easier to update if you decide to change your job objective at a later date.
- Have several people that you respect review your résumé and provide you with feedback.
- Ask them for their honest input and recommendations for improvement.

PREPARE THOROUGHLY FOR YOUR JOB INTERVIEWS

Output: You are prepared to ensure a successful interview.

The interview can be an exciting but nerve-racking time. It is your opportunity to prove your ability, experience, knowledge, and enthusiasm for the position.

When you get the interview, that means that the interviewer perceives that you may be good enough to perform the job, or else you wouldn't be called into the interviewer's office. So if you don't get the job, it may be because you were not prepared, or because you did not convey to the interviewer your qualities and strengths as they pertain to the specific business's needs.

Thoughtful planning and preparation for an interview will not only help you feel more confident, but will also prepare you to ensure a successful interview and ultimately leave a great impression on the person interviewing you.

Once you've received the call from an employer inviting you in for an interview, the real preparation begins.

The interview is really not all about you, but about the prospective employer and its need to run a successful business, make money, and/or provide a service.

Prepare Thoroughly for Your Job Interviews

1. Plan a step-by-step interview strategy including the following:
    a. How to differentiate yourself for each opportunity, stay in frequent contact, and have better planned contacts
    b. A set of criteria to use in your decision-making process (within a certain geographical range, within a certain industry, etc.)
    c. Incorporate examples of how you work harder and smarter to achieve your goals in tough times.
2. Prepare a list of questions you want to ask during the interview.
3. Be prepared to tell the employer what you're reading and learning, and that you'd like to continue doing so.
4. Practice interviewing and obtain feedback from people who have extensive experience interviewing others.
5. Develop your personal pitch. Many structured interviews, particularly those at large companies, start with a question like, "Tell me about yourself."
    a. Relax, breathe slowly, and loosen up your vocal cords.
    b. Share your relevant background.
    c. List your relevant accomplishments.
    d. Summarize why you want to work at the company and what your future professional goals are.
6. Be prepared to respond to questions about problems you have encountered in the past and how you handled them. You may also be given a hypothetical situation and asked what you would do.
    - Interviewers basically want to know how you'll perform when faced with obstacles in the position you're interviewing for.
7. Be prepared to give honest, detailed examples from your past, even if the question is hypothetical.

8. You might find yourself listing facts—if so, remember sometimes you need to tell a story. Some questions you might be asked include the following:
   - o "Describe a time you had to work with someone you didn't like."
   - o "Tell me about a time when you had to stick by a decision you had made, even though it made you very unpopular."
   - o "Give an example of something particularly innovative that you have produced that made a difference in the workplace."
   - o "How would you handle an employee who's consistently late?"
9. Focus on how the employer will benefit by how you can help do the following:
   - Create additional sources of revenue
   - Save them money
   - Streamline work processes
   - Bring overall value to the organization

> **Important: Being prepared is the key to a successful interview.**

Your credentials are first and foremost, but employers can usually tell if you are right for the job within the first two minutes of an interview.

10. Stick to the Boy Scout motto. "Be prepared," and you will be ready to impress.

11. Check up on yourself online. Do a Google search on your name. If you find something undesirable, try to have it removed.

12. Clean up what you can, and check your privacy settings on social networks. If you find something you can't get off the Internet, you should consider talking to the interviewer about it.

Prepare Thoroughly for Your Job Interviews

13. Polish your communication skills to sell yourself and calm your nerves.
    - Written skills
    - Verbal skills
    - Nonverbal skills

14. Dress appropriately to create **the right impression** and to fit in with the people who work at the organization where you will be interviewing.

15. Do your homework.
    - Remember to check the company website for basic information and for news releases.

16. Practice.
    - When you finally get through to HR, ensure you know what you want to say and that you do so clearly and confidently.
    - What type of job/position are you searching for?
    - In what division or department are you looking for a position?
    - What experience have you had?
    - What can you offer the company?

17. Make a note of your answers and have these in front of you when you make the call. You may only get a minute or two, so ensure you make a good impression.

18. Be willing to spend some time learning about the job and the people that work there, to find out what will help you fit in with the environment.

19. Be prepared to drive the conversation.
    - Too many people sit and wait to be asked questions.
    - A little small talk starts things off well.

20. Anticipate challenging questions.
    - Be prepared to be asked to identify your weaknesses.

- Identify a challenge briefly, and then discuss how you solved the problem.
- Document some standard answers to anticipated questions so you can speak fluently.

21. Work with someone in your network to rehearse being asked questions and providing your answers, ahead of all interviews.
    - Practice answering those tough questions, or even basic ones, aloud.
    - Ask for feedback from your network interviewer regarding how well he or she thinks you responded to the questions.
    - Ask for suggestions on how to improve your responses.

22. Realize a potential job lead could be anywhere.
    - Continuously utilize your network.
    - Don't be afraid to mention your occupational aspirations to your friends, family, and the rest of your network.

23. Surf job boards for more than just open positions. Job boards can be gold mines for job research.
    - You might see companies you didn't know of before.
    - Add these to your list of targets.
    - You might see the same requirements again and again. This indicates a standard for the job you want, so incorporate these items into your pitch and cover letters.

24. Invest adequate time and effort into filling out job applications.

25. Spend time to make your résumé the best possible written advertisement of yourself.

26. Obviously, all correspondence should be free of errors and typos.
    - Before sending off the application packet, look at the job posting one last time to ensure all desired material is included.

Prepare Thoroughly for Your Job Interviews

27. Do your homework.
    - Know something about potential employers.
    - Learn what you can by doing a Google search on a company to check out its financial statements.
    - Use the information to enhance your correspondence.

28. Know that employers do their homework as well.
    - Some companies require recruiters to research job applicants online, so be sure you know what they'll find.

29. Check out recent news articles related to the organization to which you are applying.

30. Utilize other websites, forums, and service review sites to find out as much information as you can about the company.

31. Whether you are interviewing for an officer-level job or a job at McDonald's, what you bring to your interview is critical.
    - The most important thing you can bring to the interview is a portfolio you put together showcasing all of your accomplishments in your career.

32. If you have an iPad or tablet, bring it with you to the interview.

33. Treat your interview like a homework assignment and do plenty of research before you shake your first hand.

34. Be prepared to ask and answer questions about the company.

35. To deal with nerves that can take over, bring a professional-looking portfolio with key points you want to mention, questions, and bullet points.
    - Used correctly, an iPad or tablet will help you demonstrate your work to the employers and show your ability to adapt to new technology.

- Showing applications you have developed and other information sets you apart and helps demonstrate your abilities.
- Information looks more visually appealing on a tablet than on a piece of paper.

> **Note: The number one complaint many interviewers have about job candidates is that they don't know enough about the company. In the eyes of some employers, a lack of research means you are not really serious about the position.**

36. Prior to an interview, research the company and read all you can find about it, its business goals, and its initiatives so you can not only answer questions but have questions ready to ask the hiring manager as well.

37. Let the company know what you could do for it.

38. Learn as much as you can about the organization.

39. Understand company initiatives to demonstrate your interest and dedication to the organization.

40. To gain an insider's perspective, browse LinkedIn and industry publications and look for new interviews with key executives.

41. Search for relevant news articles about the company and the industry.

42. Research the company on its website to help you understand what challenges may be present in the industry.

43. Google the CEO, check out the stock price (if it is a public company), and even look at an analyst's report or the annual report.

Prepare Thoroughly for Your Job Interviews

44. Based on what you learn, create a three-month, six-month, and year-long career development plan that addresses your personal and career development needs and interests.

> **Note: Constructing a plan for your role in the position demonstrates initiative, hard work, and your ability to plan ahead.**

45. Make sure you take a neat and orderly briefcase to the interview. It demonstrates that you are organized and implies that your work will be neat and clean and that you are prepared in all areas to get a job and to work.

46. Be prepared to consider a temporary position for the time being.
    - Managers sometimes offer positions on a temporary or temp-to-permanent basis to see if you can prove yourself on the job.
    - Not only will a temporary position pay some bills, it may be an audition for a potential permanent position, or at least a way to get a good reference for another position.

47. Be prepared to demonstrate a positive attitude through telephone calls and in interviews. By being positive and seeing each position as an opportunity, it will happen.

48. **Do not** put yourself in a position to be stumped going into the interview.

49. Create a matrix including questions that could be asked during the interview, your answers to the questions, and examples to support your answers.

50. Have your responses ready as soon as each question is asked.

51. Provide complete, relevant answers to questions that go beyond the surface level that will allow the interviewer to make an objective evaluation of your ability to perform the job.

52. You will probably be asked in the beginning of the interview something like, "Why are you applying for this position?" or "Tell me about yourself."
    - It may be the easiest question you will be asked, and is usually the most overlooked question in preparation. It also has the most relevance because it is part of the crucial first impression.
    - The type of job you are seeking answers why you are there.

53. Prepare a one-to-two minute monologue that includes the following:
    - Education and training (answers why your skills are relevant to the job)
    - Experience (answers why you are qualified)
    - Strengths and skills (answers why you are unique to the position)

54. Be prepared when asked questions that focus on the business model of a company/agency or the products and services of a company/agency.
    - Know something about the company and/or department that you are interviewing with.
    - Know the mission and vision of an organization, why they exist, where they are going, and everything else you can find.

55. Go into the interviews knowing what a behavioral-based interview is and how it is conducted.
    - A behavioral-based interview is based on discovering how the interviewee acts in specific employment-related situations.

56. Respond to behavioral-based questions by providing specific examples of your accomplishments, actions, and achievements.

57. Do understand that employers that conduct behavioral-based interviews assume that your previous behavior will determine future behavior.

58. Be prepared to identify when you are being asked a behavioral-based question.
    - Behavioral questions usually come in a form like, "Tell me about a situation in which you…" or "Describe a problem you were faced with and how you dealt with it."
    - Include the following information when answering these type of questions:
        1. Situation: Describe the situation with relevant detail.
        2. Tasks: What were the tasks that you had to overcome or complete?
        3. Actions: What actions did you take to accomplish the tasks?
        4. Result: What were the end results, and what did you learn? (Make sure this is positive.)

59. Focus on the **strengths** that have relevance to the position you are applying for.

60. Identify weaknesses that the interviewer may already perceive and address them by turning them into assets.
    - An example would be interviewing for a position that requires experience with leading other employees, and your résumé lacks direct supervisory experience.
    - Mention that with a focus on what makes it into a personal strength: "A weakness for me as it pertains to this position is my lack of direct supervisory experience. However, in a previous position, I served as a temporary supervisor over other employees."

61. Answer every question as though the fundamental reason why the interviewer is asking you is to answer the ultimate question: Why should I hire **you**?

62. Look at the interview in its entirety and prepare for it and approach it as though it is an exchange of ideas. Your interviewers are trying to get to know you, and you should be trying to get to know them. Ultimately their decision is going to be based on fit. Are you a good fit? And if yes, why should I hire **you**?

63. When offered an opportunity to ask them questions, make sure you have questions ready.

64. The interview is where you and an employer get to know each other. Think of it like a first date.
    - While a job interview is in a professional setting and the outcomes are different, the intentions are the same.
    - You've exchanged information because you think there might be a connection, and now you're ready for your second date.
    - As much as you want to make a good first impression, the employer needs to make a good impression as well.

65. Just like when you are on a first date, you don't want one person to dominate the conversation and ask all the questions.
    - It should be a balanced dialogue, and you should ask questions that get to the heart of the matter: Who is this employer, what are their values, and why should I work for this company?

66. Before the interview, write down things that you want to remember during the interview.
    - In all situations where people become fearful, their thinking gets a little fuzzy.
    - Know exactly what you want to ask and jot down any reminders about nervous habits that you have. For example, "Don't fidget."

67. Beforehand, anticipate a few likely problems the company could have. For example, they could have problems with sales or client relations.
    - Then memorize your accomplishment stories in advance so you can easily retell them.
    - The more specific you are, the better.

68. Be mentally prepared to interview with one interviewer and/or a team of interviewers.
    - You may interview with a team in just one interview.
    - You may interview with several teams in several interviews.
    - You may interview several times with same interview team.

69. Bring written materials about the company to the interview. It shows initiative, intelligence, research skills, and the understanding that you are choosing the company just as much as the company is choosing you.

70. Staying on top of the company and the industry will help you succeed not only in the interview, but it will help you if you are offered the position.

TEST YOUR STRATEGIC AND TACTICAL PLANS

Now that you have created a strategic and tactical plan, it is time to test your plans to see if there needs to be any adjustment along the way. The following steps are designed to guide you through your testing and adjustment process.

1. Identify potential job opportunities.
2. Continuously increase the quantity of the prospects you are working on.
3. Research the company prior to making a cold call.
    - Is it a large or small organization?
    - Does it have branch offices?
    - What are its strongest products and/or services?
    - In what areas is it weak?
4. Look in newspapers.
5. Look on the Internet.
6. Ask your network and support systems for possible opportunities.

7. Determine the name of the person you should call. That may be the person who works in the human resources (HR) department, or it may be someone in the operations part of the company.
   - Search the company's website.
   - Call the company's switchboard.
   - Complete and submit job applications.

8. Use placement agencies.
   - Never go to just one agency.
   - Always go to as many as possible.
   - It is easy, and it increases your chances a lot!

9. Perform cold calls.
   - Locate a specific person who can help you (usually the human resources or hiring manager at a company or organization you're interested in).

10. Call that person and ask if they are hiring, but do not become discouraged if they are not.

11. Ask what kind of qualifications they look for, or if they have apprentice or government-sponsored work programs.

12. Ask if you can send your résumé indicating what field you want to go into.

13. Indicate whether you would accept a lesser job and work your way up to the job you really want.

14. Respond to opportunities by scheduling interviews.

15. Keep your options open.
    - It is perfectly OK to have several irons in the fire at the same time.
    - Apply and interview for multiple positions.

- Don't wait until one position interview plays out completely before applying for other positions.
- Continue your job search before you know for sure if you do or don't get an offer from the first interview.
- Diversify the risk and disappointment that is inevitable when any single opportunity disappears.
- By keeping your options open, you present yourself as a more passionate and energetic candidate.
- You are then in the flow of information and ideas, and that makes you more valuable to your future employer.

16. **Do not** turn up your nose at job descriptions. All interview experience is good experience.

IMPLEMENT YOUR EXECUTION PLAN: NAIL THE INTERVIEW

Output: Leave a great impression on the person interviewing you.

1. Begin your interview process by making a very **good first impression.**
2. Focus on the fact that employers want and need employees who are passionate, confident, and energized, and who can contribute to the accomplishment of their business goals

> **Note: Some prospective employers do not care as much about your credentials or your experience as they do about what you can do for them right then.**

3. Look and act like a professional.
   a. The easiest product in the world to sell is the product you believe in 100 percent. If you are not confident that you can sell yourself to a particular company, don't waste anyone's time. You need to believe it, and they'll believe it.
   b. Believe in yourself. If you believe in your abilities, the interviewer is much more likely to believe in your abilities as well.
   c. Arrive on time.
   d. Dress appropriately.

e. Go to the interview alone and not with friends or family.
f. Talk and listen.
g. **Do not** go into the interview with a sense of entitlement. There is a fine line between confident and arrogant.
h. Mind your manners.
i. Bring your résumé, paper, pen, and a business card. Consider each part an important addition to your interview arsenal.
j. Use compelling evidence to convince the interview team that they need to hire you.
k. Don't beg.
l. Make a strong value proposition that is based on what you know about the organization.
m. Play to their needs and wants when you meet with them.

4. Demonstrate that you really want the job.
    a. Focus on the needs of the employer and demonstrate how you are perfect for this particular position.
    b. When given the opportunity, explain how you can benefit the organization.

5. Show enthusiasm during the job interview.
    a. Always make certain the company you're interviewing with feels as if it is your first choice, no matter what other companies are involved in your job search.

6. **Do not** get ahead of yourself.
    a. As much as you may be dying to know about promotions, raises, and vacation time, don't jump the gun and tackle these issues during the first interview.
    b. Focus on landing the position, then on whether the package is suitable.

Implement Your Execution Plan: Nail the Interview

7. Visualize yourself in a job where you feel **confident and efficient**, and try to project that attitude during your interview.

8. Remember to breathe. Take a few slow deep breaths before and during the interview. It will help you slow your heart rate, lower your blood pressure, and reduce your adrenaline flow.

9. Make good eye contact to demonstrate confidence. Looking away or down signals a lack of confidence.

10. Smile and be pleasant.
    a. Plan to share an appropriate and relevant story that will prompt a smile.
    b. All things being equal, people will always choose the person who is most likable.

11. Use the interviewer's name and the name of others involved in the conversation during the interview. In addition, use their names in follow-up e-mails and conversations.

12. Demonstrate your **listening** skills.
    a. Show that you are really listening.
    b. **Do not** get so focused on creating the next right response that you miss out on what is most important to your potential employer.

13. Take advantage of any opportunities that ask you to paraphrase what your interviewer has shared.

14. Look interested. It indicates that you are engaged. Small nonverbal behavior can convey the message that you are listening.
    a. A slight tilt of the head or a quick eyebrow arch can communicate interest.

How to Get the Job

   b. To a somewhat limited degree, tactfully mirror some of the behaviors of your interviewer.
   c. They may be speaking softly, so you might want to speak somewhat softly as well.
   d. Be careful not to go too far and offend the interviewers.
15. Demonstrate tempered panache.
    a. Panache is a French-origin word that represents courage and a dashing manner with style or limited swagger.
    b. Example: Walk into the interview with panache.
16. Don't take all the credit or exaggerate your own contributions. It comes off as very self-serving and egotistical, and will not make you look like a team player.
17. When asked to describe your strengths and weaknesses, be accountable and humble.
    a. Don't blame co-workers for failures, and don't dress up your strengths.
    b. Be humble and convey the message that you hold yourself to high standards.
18. Don't rush.
    a. Don't let nerves make you rush through an answer just to have it done and over with.
    b. Slow down and speak in a normal conversational tone that allows your interviewer to hear and understand your answers.
19. Don't mention that you are nervous. It might leave your interviewer looking for flaws.
20. Demonstrate sincere interest in the interviewer.
    a. Pay attention to what your interviewer is interested in.

    b. Listen carefully to what they say.
    c. Think about what they say.
    d. Respond to what they say.
21. If you are not sure you understand a question, ask for clarification.
    a. Depending on the question, it might be helpful to ask for an example.
22. Take a moment before answering questions. If you feel you need a moment, say something like, "Let me think about that for a moment."
23. Come up with three points about yourself that you consider strengths.
    a. Be specific.
    b. If one of your strengths is helping people, provide succinct examples.
24. During the interview, cite specific things about the company that appeal to you, or ask specific questions.
25. Explain why you are a good match for this particular company and industry and what you can bring to the party.
26. Communicate that you want to contribute to the company as much as you can.
27. When asked a question, answer the question and be relatively succinct.
    a. Don't go on and on when answering questions.
    b. After answering the question, ask the interviewer, "Did I answer your question?" You might be surprised how often the response is no.
    c. Don't ask too many questions because it makes you seem desperate.
    d. Don't ask the wrong or inappropriate questions.
28. Think about your goals first.
    - Don't feel obligated to walk into the interview with a set number of questions.

- Asking the first question will make you stand out from the 99 percent who sit nervously waiting to be peppered with questions.
- Think of the questions in terms of your career and personal goals.
- If you're moving into a role with more responsibility, think about how that will affect what questions you ask.
- If you're starting a family soon, what do you want to know about the company's commitment to work/life balance?
- Don't wait till the end to ask your questions.
- In fact, aim for a fifty-fifty split; match each question you receive with one of your own.
- This is supposed to be a dialogue, not an interrogation.

Questions You Should Ask

- "Would it be OK if I take notes?" If the interviewer says yes, then take out your notepad and take plenty of notes, so when you write your follow-up letter, you'll have more than enough information to include.

> **Caution:** Do not take so many notes that you lose eye contact with the interviewer.

Ask the following:

- What keeps you up at night?
- What are your biggest business issues?
- How do you measure success?
- What are some of the ways your company encourages teamwork?
- Is the company committed to promotion from within whenever possible?
- What does the company expect in the way of personal and professional growth for a person hired into this position?

- Are there paid ongoing learning and growth opportunities offered at my level of job responsibility? What obligations do I have if I elect to take advantage of them?
- How are your mission and values reflected in day-to-day life at the company? Will you share some examples with me?
- If your son, daughter, or friend were looking for a job, would you recommend working for this company? Why?
- What do you think distinguishes this company from your competitors, both from a public and from an employee perspective?
- How often do you speak with your officers? When you do, what do they normally ask you? Do they ask for your opinion?
- How does the company demonstrate a sense of pride in its employees? Can you help me understand what it looks for in return?
- Please provide examples of how the company demonstrates that they value a difference in work and personal time.
- What kind of career development programs does your company offer?
    - This demonstrates that you're interested in improving your skills and knowledge base.
    - Just because you're done with school doesn't mean you should stop learning.
    - Asking about available extracurricular programs shows that you're open to learning what the company has to teach you.
- What's the typical career path?
    - Always talk from a career standpoint.
        - Companies spend money on employee orientation and training, so they want to know that you're staying with them for more than twelve months.
    - Let them know you're in it for the long haul.

- Why did you decide to work for this company?
    - The question proves you're looking for more insight into whether or not the job is right for you.
    - Before extending an offer, employers want to know that you're confident you'll mesh with the company both professionally and personally.

29. Don't make the mistake of not asking any questions! A quiet candidate is a boring candidate.

30. Make your pitch regarding what you can do to help when appropriate.
    - It should be a direct response to your potential employer's needs and problems.
    - Get to the heart of a problem and sell your solutions.
    - If they say they have a real problem with X, tell a story about how you solved X at your old job and how it will work again.
    - Accomplishment stories are the best way to showcase your experience.

31. State your interest in the job—a no-brainer that's commonly skipped.
    - Say something that shows you've digested the conversation: "After learning more about this opportunity, I'm very interested and confident that I'd be an excellent fit."

32. Ask for the position, follow up, and offer thanks.
    - You need to ask for the job.
    - At the end of the interview, sum up your strengths. Tell the interviewer that you are excited about the position, and say, "I would really like to contribute to this company. I am hoping you select me."

33. Express your enthusiasm and your willingness to do anything, not just the most interesting work.

Implement Your Execution Plan: Nail the Interview

34. At the end of the interview, ask several direct questions.
    - What are my next steps in the interview process?
    - When can I follow up with you?
    - What is your time frame for making a decision?

35. Finish off the interview with a thank-you and a handshake.
    - A polite exit will leave your potential employer with a positive impression.

36. Demonstrate good business acumen.

37. There are two questions you should never ask.
    - What are the hours?
    - Do I get time off around the holidays?

Note: You didn't even get the job yet, and you will appear to be already counting down the days until a break! Bad move.

EVALUATE YOUR PERFORMANCE AFTER YOUR INTERVIEW

Output: Feedback data and reinforcement of a great impression on the person interviewing you.

1. Reflect after each interview and phone call on what went well and what did not.
2. Keep your name in the game. Many employers like to see that you are dedicated to landing the job.
    a. Leave an impressive last impression. Sending a handwritten note immediately after the interview can make all the difference in getting a job or not.
    b. Drop your interviewer a four-to-eight sentence note of thanks letting him or her know that you appreciated the opportunity. Reiterate your interest and that you look forward to hearing from the interviewer.
    c. Complete a tactful follow-up by phone.

Evaluate Your Performance after Your Interview

> **Caution:**
> - Avoid incessant follow-up calling or e-mailing.
> - Do not be too verbose. You don't want to appear to be desperate and needy for a job.

4. Determine if you need to get some additional training to break into your chosen field.
   - Just because you may not have been successful in your job search so far does not mean you cannot get a good job. Sometimes it only means that you need to become further prepared to do so.

5. If you are rejected for a job, still send a thank-you note to thank the employer for the opportunity and wish them well. When the next opportunity comes around, you will increase the probability that they will remember you.

6. If you are disillusioned with finding a job and prefer to start working for yourself, see the next section on starting your own company.

Good Practices for Keeping a Job

Getting the Job is the first step. Keeping the job is just as important and requires different skills and behaviors. The following proven steps can help you keep the job you have worked so hard to get.

1. Learn what you need to produce a valuable output as soon as possible.

2. Demonstrate ethical behavior at all times.

3. Be at the job when needed, especially during the first ninety days.

4. Don't be first to offer to go home.

5. Demonstrate a positive attitude at all times.

6. Leave your troubles at home.

7. Don't talk badly about other co-workers.

8. Realize you are being paid to provide a service, produce a product, and maybe for your expertise—not just for being there collecting hours.

9. Recognize that not all employees are interchangeable or equal. Make yourself one of the valuable ones.

10. Do more than expected.

11. The fact that you are being paid to be there means what you do is important to what is being produced.

12. The quality of what you do, no matter big or small, is reflected in that end result. Look at the big picture.

13. Do your very best at any job. If your job is digging a ditch, then be the best ditchdigger there ever will be. You may have many jobs throughout your life, but doing your best sets the standard of your work ethic that will follow you in everything you do. It is your personal bar, so set it very high.

14. Don't be lazy—be proactive and demonstrate initiative.

15. Energy channeled in the right direction breeds success. It often takes one set of skills to get a job and a different set of skills to keep a job.

SECTION 2
Steps to Start and Sustain Your Own Business

> "Find your passion, get good at it, develop a business plan, and know you'll get rich slowly."
>
> "Entrepreneurship is a case for the tortoise and not the hare."
>
> Joe Harless

Output that will be produced at the end of this section:

- A start-up business plan that provides focus and direction, enables good decision making, and increases the probability of producing an entity that shields your assets and protects your business

- Signed client and customer contracts

- Strong client and customer relationships

- Financial self-reliance and independence

How to Get the Job

- An investment

- A management and organization plan

- Useful data about you and your new business

- A strategic business plan

- Funding

- Marketing plan data

- An excellence model for your company

- Financial strategy plan data

- An exit strategy

In this current economy, a job isn't just a job. At this time, according to the Bureau of Labor Statistics, some 205 million full-time jobs have evaporated in the last thirteen months. Managers are now often turning to outsourcing. A new generation of workers has 24–7 connectivity.

Some workers have good reason to lack loyalty and think like mavericks. Some are now writers, photographers, musicians, and other creative types who are starting their own businesses. There is a spread of independent work to higher-income professions not known for their creativity like law, finance, contractors, and human resources.

New entrants are moving into owning their own business. Some employers no longer want to be saddled with paying benefits like vacation time and health insurance.

Many people are now building their own lifestyles. Some people are going back to a guild mentality. There are new companies like Elance.com or snagajob.com. These can help you start a new profession in part-time or contract-based work.

Steps to Start and Sustain Your Own Business

> **Caution:** Be careful in going in this direction, because you could be a highly qualified person who is not good at the business side of selling yourself. You can hit slow periods where a project ends before another is lined up. There is not a safety net for independent workers, so you need to be prepared with a savings plan with rainy-day funds.
>
> The Freelancers Union provides benefits for independent workers. In a freelance-based job market, talented, skilled, and energetic people can still do great work and make a good living.

Have you decided to create your own future under your own terms, maybe via the World Wide Web? Have you decided to control your own destiny from now on?

Many start-up companies fail within the first two years. Learn how to create and **sustain a business over the long term**.

To succeed in starting your own business you need to be smart and prepared. Get educated on the basics to avoid the ready-fire-aim approach to starting your own business.

The **basics** provided in the following information prepare you to minimize rework and reduce cost by ensuring that you take the approach of ready-aim-fire, and at the same time increase your probability of success.

> "Analysis and design is worth a pound of brainstorming."
> **Joe Harless**

Analysis

1. Perform your due diligence.

2. Assess and analyze yourself to see if you are the kind of person who should start a business of your own.
    - Do you work well without supervision?
    - Do you desire freedom, authenticity, accountability, and self-defined success?
    - Have you demonstrated significant self-confidence, tenacity, perseverance, stick-to-it-tiveness, and an excellent work ethic?
    - Do you have self-confidence and a positive attitude?
    - Do you have enough guts and courage to be successful?
    - Are you willing to risk everything to make your business successful?
    - Do your goals include creating equity, controlling your own future, enhancing your income, and setting your own hours?
    - Are you good at creating and managing a business system and the work processes within that system?
    - Are you the kind of person who chooses to make your own luck?
    - Are you good at marketing yourself and your business?
    - Are you good at leading people and managing processes?
    - Are you able to follow a plan but adapt and adjust your plan as needed, sometimes on the fly?
    - Do you have a vision and a good business plan?
    - Do you currently have a significant support network established that can support you along the way?
        - Friends
        - Family
        - Co-workers

- Community organizations
- Chamber of Commerce
- Professional advisor
- Do you have **sufficient resources** to get you through the start-up and eventual slow times?
- Are you capable of being an independent worker who operates under your own terms, untethered to a large organization, serving multiple clients and customers?

If you answered yes to the preceding questions, and if your vision and goals include starting your own company, then begin shaping and sharpening your focus by creating a business concept and a business plan. The business plan will provide focus for everything else you do. If you need investors, the first thing they will want to see is your business plan.

> **Remember: "A business plan is vital to success—and melts the icy heart of a banker, somewhat."**
>
> **Joe Harless**

Use your responses to the following items to create your business plan:

1. Define the industry and business. Create definitions of your business and organization, ensuring a common understanding of who you are and what you do.

2. Begin by documenting answers to the following questions:
    - What is your vision?
    - What business will you be in?
    - What do you really want to **produce as an end result** of your business? Is it money and security, goodwill, service to others, a better world?
    - Do you understand the technical aspects of your target market and the market conditions including supply and demand conditions?

- What is your strategy in planning your next steps?
- Do you plan to be working as an independent (maybe a home-based business)?
- Do you plan to be a large business, a small business, or a microbusiness (maybe two or three people)?
- What type of business organization structure (or entity) is best for you? Each has its own advantages and disadvantages. Consult with your accountant and/or attorney as to your choice of entity.
  - C corporation
  - S corporation
  - Sole proprietorship
  - Limited liability company (LLC)
  - Limited partnership (LP)
  - General partnership
  - Personalized services company
  - Franchise

Note: There are numerous tax advantages and protections provided by incorporating. The income tax rate of a corporation is less than individual income tax rates, and some expenses can be paid with pretax dollars within the corporation.

- What products and/or services will you provide to customers?
- What technical and special assistance is required by your customers?
- Customers: Who uses your products and services?
- Scope: In what parts of the country or the world will you compete?
- What process will you use to look for customers and suppliers?
- Target markets: In what ways will your products and services be used?

- How will you create your brand?
- What kind of culture will you create?
- What kind of people will you hire?
- How safe and responsible will you be for the environment you affect, including communities and governments?
- Functions: What is your role in providing those products and services?
- Business and work system: Identify your overall work system, work processes, input, output, receiving system, and feedback systems.
- Work processes: How will you move from vertical product-thinking to horizontal process-thinking?
  - Flow-chart your work processes.
  - How will you manage the critical interactions and interdependencies between the work processes?
  - Flow-chart your customers' work processes to identify opportunities where you can provide solutions to help them achieve their business goals and objectives.
  - If you need more information on creating or improving work systems and processes, reference my web site: dougmead.com.

3. Involve all qualified personnel in verbal, visual, and quantitative business data that flows continually.

4. Interpret this data from the perspective of your customers and suppliers.

5. Identify your skills, knowledge, and information needs. Your greatest assets are your education and the education of the people who work for you.

6. What skills and knowledge do the people you hire need to demonstrate?

7. Perform a skills/knowledge/information **gap analysis.**

8. Identify a list of business skills/knowledge/information required to be a successful business owner. Examples include the following:
    - Business law because it is too expensive to be ignorant of the law. If you are designing new products, learn patent law to keep from being sued.
    - The **financial** elements of running your business
    - Financial aptitude/intelligence
        - The difference between an asset and a liability. Assets put money in your bank account. Liabilities take money out of your bank account.
        - How to measure income and expenses and how to balance assets against liabilities
        - How to know where your cash is flowing
        - Sophisticated accounting analysis
        - How to interpret and understand your financial data, what the data really mean, and what the data are telling you
        - The art of business financial intelligence
        - How to critically evaluate your company and use numbers and financial tools to make and analyze decisions
        - How to interpret what the accounting and financial numbers **really** mean
            - Profitability ratios
            - Leverage ratios
            - Liquidity ratios
            - Efficiency ratios
            - Return on investment
            - Financial strategies
    - How financial statements work—they are the key to knowing how to improve your company's financial performance.
    - How financial success is measured and how you and anyone else in the organization have an impact on the company's performance

- Practical ways to use financial statements to create your company
- How to gain insights into the assumptions, estimates, and biases in the financial numbers
- The right mix for blending finances with the often-subjective art of impacting the bottom line
- How to interpret an income statement
- How to interpret balance sheets
- How to interpret cash-flow reports and how cash connects with everything else
- How to **interpret financial analysis and the big picture**
- How to speak the financial language
- Know which questions to ask
- How to use financial information
- How to use limited data to come as close as possible to an accurate description of how well your company is performing at all times
- The difference between revenue and sales
- Know the methods of valuation
- The skills of marketing, sales, distribution, advertising, and copywriting
- Public relations
- How to get free publicity
- How to interpret corporate, state, and national rules and regulations
- How to lead employees and manage work processes
- How to perform customer and supplier intelligence
- How to perform surveys, collect data from focus groups, and continually collect data from all the interactions between your suppliers and your customers
- How to ensure observation of your customers directly regarding how they currently operate by people with the necessary technical and business expertise

9. Place a check next to the business skills/knowledge/information required to be a successful business owner that you already possess and can demonstrate.

10. Place an X next to the business skills/knowledge/information you **do not** have at this time but will help you be successful.

11. Attend classes, obtain work experience, and/or gain input from your support network to obtain the skills/knowledge/information you need as soon as possible.

12. Take the time to learn financial literacy from exemplary performers who have demonstrated success in starting up their own companies.

13. Identify your infrastructure, or your support network. Examples include the following:
    - Attorney
    - CPA (get an exemplary accountant)
    - Bank
    - Credit union
    - An exemplary financial expert

14. Identify your expected volume growth over the planning horizon.

15. Determine your work location (office, home office, etc.).

16. Determine what technologies you need to operate your business.
    - The Internet—register your name as a domain. For example, dougmead.com. Now my e-mail can be doug@dougmead.com.
    - Office-supply superstores
    - The post office

DESIGN AN EXIT STRATEGY AS ONE COMPONENT OF YOUR BUSINESS PLAN

Output: Maximize the price paid by the ultimate buyer of your company with the best terms possible.

Every company needs an exit strategy. A good exit strategy should
- improve the probabilities of success,
- shorten the time to exit, and
- significantly increase the ultimate exit valuation.

Every manager within your system needs to know the exit strategy.

The entire purpose of most companies and investors is to maximize the price paid by the ultimate buyer.

The company's operation is simply a system with the input being entrepreneurs' effort and investors' cash. The most significant output is often the purchase price paid by the ultimate buyer.

1. Begin with the end in mind. Now is the time to think about and design what your exit strategy will be when you decide to take the next step in your journey.

2. Determine what you want to do in the future.
    - Do you plan to sell your business, pass it on to your children, transition to a passive ownership role, or maybe just let it fade away?
3. If you need external investment, design and produce and be prepared to sign your exit strategy before the first dollar of external investment goes into the company.
4. Treat selling a company as a business process.

> **Note: Done well, the exit process often can make more money for the owner or shareholders than any other process during the company's lifetime because it monetizes all the work and investment that went into designing and creating the company. Designing and executing the exit strategy well can easily increase the entire value of your business by 50 percent or more.**

5. Acknowledge and appreciate the degree to which different types of investors are only compatible with certain exit strategies.
6. Make your simple exit strategy a required prerequisite to designing your financing strategy.
7. Clarify your **exit strategy up front** so that you can build your business with the end in mind.
8. Clearly articulate the desired outcome as a business goal and include a price and a date.
9. Sign off the exit strategy.
10. Plan the intermediate steps needed to achieve the goal.

Design an Exit Strategy as One Component of Your Business Plan

11. Demonstrate regard for the quality of the organization that will be left behind after you exit the business.

12. Ensure alignment between the types of investors and the exit strategy.

13. Look at your business through the eyes of an ultimate buyer at all times, and you'll see the essential steps you need to follow to develop a more valuable business.

14. Ensure you have a key branding or other protections from competitors in your market space.

15. Have a solid and growing sales pipeline.

16. Review regular progress by conducting your own buyer's audit of your business.

17. Build your business so that you can sell it for the price you have identified.

18. Monitor and pay close attention to your system and work processes.

19. Over time, decrease the business's dependence on you the owner.

20. Ensure you have strong controls in place.

21. Have a sales system that guarantees future growth and reliable income streams.

PERFORM A DUE-DILIGENCE BUSINESS AUDIT

A good due-diligence business audit should

- improve the probability of selling your business,
- shorten the time to process the sale, and
- significantly maximize the ultimate valuation of your business when you sell it in the future.

As a potential buyer, you need to perform due diligence that includes a rigorous analysis of a business, focusing on accounting, legal, marketing, and other technical areas to best determine the financial value in a few weeks or months.

Be prepared for both financial and strategic buyers.

Financial Buyers

- Look for businesses they can buy in which they can finance half or more of the purchase price, and that have sufficient cash flow to repay that debt
- Focus on the business's cash flow because they borrow money for a part of the purchase price
- Very carefully scrutinize your recast financial data

Perform a Due-Diligence Business Audit

- Tend to value a business by using a multiple of three to six times earnings before interest and taxes, after making adjustments for expenses that would not continue for a new owner
- Deduct from the purchase price any interest-bearing debt they will assume

Strategic Buyers

- Have somewhat different reasons for wanting to purchase a business than financial buyers do
- Are often interested in businesses that will offer a synergy with their other existing businesses
- Look for a business that offers more value than just the official valuation
- May be willing to pay a premium price

> **Caution: Strategic buyers may actually be inquiring about your business because they intend to use your financial information to compete against you.**

As a business owner, you need to prepare for the sale transaction by monetizing a piece of your life through your financial reporting.

Compile financial statements so you can represent the company's financial position.

1. Prepare to ease a future transaction and earn trust from a potential buyer by organizing high-quality financial records. Present your business in the best possible light by making sure your books are
   - accurate,
   - well-organized,
   - easy to understand, and
   - forthright and honest.

How to Get the Job

2. Be prepared for a buyer's due-diligence representative, bankers who are financing a purchase, and your investment banker's request for three to four years of records organized on a monthly basis. Reports typically requested include the following:
   - Trial balances
   - Customer sales registers
   - Account details
   - Payroll records
   - Tax returns
   - Gross profit (and return on assets) by activity or product line
   - Financial projections and a business plan that reflects your company's management
   - The honest reason you are selling the business

3. Ensure you have these records in an easy-to-navigate repository, so you can provide a potential buyer with information necessary to establish a historical context for your business.

4. To have a positive effect on the price a buyer is willing to pay for your company, perform an audit of your financial statements in addition to performing financial reporting to file your tax returns.
   - Prepare, or have someone else prepare, an audit or review opinion on your statements to raise the standard of the financial information.

5. Maintain financial-statement accounting records using both cash and the accrual basis, or convert to simply an accrual basis. The cash basis reports revenue when earned and expenses when obligations are incurred. An accrual basis is a more standard month-end close statement.

6. Proactively arrange your financial information, although buyers will most likely perform their own buy-side due diligence. Either prepare yourself or pay a sell-side firm to perform a sell-side due diligence.
   - One of the advantages of financial audits compiled or reviewed by a reputable accounting firm is that they should strengthen your position in the negotiations and allow you to negotiate better terms, since the financial information is considered objective and trustworthy.
7. Be sure you are prepared to provide timely and accurate information during the due-diligence process.
8. Be prepared to answer questions about sales, profits, expenses depreciation, inventory valuation, and every other aspect of the financials.
9. Design a thoughtful presentation of the business to capture the value you have created, increasing the probability of getting your sale price.
10. Prepare a selling document that describes your company, containing the information needed for a buyer to determine if they are interested in pursuing a purchase. If the buyer is interested, they will then ask for more detailed information.

CONSIDER A FRANCHISE BUSINESS

In addition to the prior tasks and steps required for starting your own business, make sure you are ready to wear all the hats an entrepreneur must wear.

- Make sure you are well capitalized prior to purchasing a franchise.

- Assess and demonstrate your natural sales skills and your ability to interact with customers.

- Carefully research and get information about how to buy into a franchise.

- Franchising may be a good choice for entrepreneurs looking for strong corporate brand support.

- Follow a franchiser's proven formula and the company's business model.

- Take advantage of the corporate tools, support, track record, brand reputation, and sometimes direct or third-party financing to reach your business goals.

- Take advantage of training that is provided.

- Take advantage of licenses and other management training tools.

- Get skilled in the core competencies.

- Shadow licensees to learn what works and what does not work for them.
- Use the brand's road map and then add your own entrepreneurial skills.
- Work hard to deliver valuable products and services to your customers.
- Use the franchise model to grow your brand.
- Identify, research, assess, and anticipate your competition.
- Identify trends in the business market.

DESIGN AND DEVELOP AN EXCELLENCE MODEL FOR YOUR COMPANY

1. Identify how you will ensure you meet or exceed the required quality performance standards.

2. Describe the elements of your vision in more detail by specifying the clear, realistic, and attainable performance standards that best describe the conditions of the vision.

3. Determine if you, your customers, or both will identify the quality performance standards you need to consistently meet or exceed.

4. Identify how you will know if your performance standards are being met consistently.

5. Determine how will you test and track your product and services quality performance standards.

6. Identify how you will **prevent deviation** from the quality performance standards.

7. Identify your backup plan if somehow the performance standards are not being met.

Design and Develop an Excellence Model for Your Company

8. Develop a brand.

9. Create a brand mantra.

10. Example: Cost-effective human performance that results in improved business performance

11. Design and produce professional-looking stationery and business cards.

12. Create a plan to balance your work and home life.

13. Create a code of conduct that
    - identifies **legal requirements and regulations** and **the consequences** for not meeting those requirements and regulations
    - identifies your moral and ethical principles and values

14. How will you support your community, charities, and others?
    - Will you volunteer?
    - Will you make cash donations?
    - Will you hold fundraisers?

15. **Develop common goals** for the entire organization to monitor progress and measure achievements, to identify areas that require improvement, and to set performance objectives.

DEVELOP YOUR QUALITY GAP ANALYSIS

1. Identify where you would like to be in each quality performance standard.

2. Rate your current performance against each quality performance standard on a scale of one to ten.

3. Identify the gaps.

4. Identify the most important quality performance standards for immediate attention.

DESIGN AND DEVELOP YOUR FINANCIAL STRATEGY PLAN

1. Develop a list of assumptions **to develop a strong foundation**. Examples include the following:
   - You balance a variety of clients and customers.
   - You are brave enough to say no to negative-energy clients and customers.
   - You will charge by the project and not the hour.
   - You will not sell yourself short and you will charge enough. Remember, you are selling solutions to problems.
   - You have an investment strategy.

2. Make sure you hire an **exemplary certified public accountant (CPA)** to guide you in tax matters and ensure legal maximized use of the tax code to your advantage.

3. Estimate your taxes and set aside enough money to pay them

> Note: In the end, an exemplary CPA and an exemplary attorney will save you far more than what they cost. It is less expensive to pay your attorney and your accountant than to pay the government.

4. Use financial software to track your revenue and expenses.
   - Write checks
   - Produce financial reports
   - Produce invoices
   - Create and track your budget
   - Track projects
5. Develop a list of financial goals, including three-year projections of income, profit and loss, balance sheets, and cash-flow projections.
6. Identify which items would require capital funding.
7. Describe your budget.
8. Watch your overhead expenses.

> **Remember: It is not how much money you make that determines success; it is how much money you keep. Revenue without financial intelligence is money out the door.**

9. Keep all receipts.
10. Identify possible sources of funding and capital (both debt and equity).
11. Establish a line of credit. The best time to establish a line of credit is when you do not need it.
    - Credit cards
    - Investors
    - Individual public offering (IPO)
    - Microfinancing

Design and Develop Your Financial Strategy Plan

> **Caution:** You must be very careful when raising money for your business. Securities rules and regulations include both federal and state law. If you do it incorrectly, you could end up in jail.
>
> If there is a problem, the Securities and Exchange Commission (the SEC) can require you to provide the following:
> Adequate full disclosure to potential investors about the business history.
> Reasonable projections that are clearly noted as being speculative or forward looking.
> Serious discussion and warnings about the risks of investment.

12. Describe the break-even analysis.

13. Get advice from your support network to learn how to manage risk.

14. Describe your accounting controls.

15. Describe your required tax and insurance needs (health, auto, house insurance, etc.).

16. Focus on funding your own retirement plan. and put away money during prosperous times.

17. **Keep your expenses low and minimize your liabilities.**

18. Get disability insurance.

19. Put money aside to take advantage of opportunities and increase the probability of being able to survive during lean revenue-generating times.

20. Invest and reinvest your profits wisely.

21. Build a solid foundation of assets.

How to Get the Job

22. If you need investors, they will want to see documents verifying the appropriate business and legal organization of your entity, including articles of incorporation, bylaws, certification of the secretary of state (as applicable).

23. If you decide you need to sell ownership interest in your company, there are several options, depending on how you have designated your new business.

If	Then You Can
Corporation	Sell stock Note: If you decide at some point to arrange for a public offering, check in advance with your state and/or securities attorney for the most recent approval and filing requirements offering. The requirements change frequently in a number of states.
Limited partnership	Sell limited-partnership interests
Limited liability company	Sell membership interests

Design and Develop Your Financial Strategy Plan

> **Remember:**
>
> - Most investors want to realize earnings and get out the stock within a year.
> - Investors will want to see copies of a realistic financial statement of the business that shows the costs to get it going, the minimum and maximum amounts you are expecting to raise, and fair projections showing where the business will be—both at its low-end and high-end estimates—in the next six months, year, and so on.
> - The further out you project your estimates, the less reliable the forward projections will be.
> - To ensure your ethical business professionalism and full disclosure, potential investors have a right to know the truth and to be made aware of the risks.
> - For a new business, include a statement that these projections are not verifiable, that the projections may not be reached, and that the whole business may not succeed.
> - These disclosures can help you get prudent investors.

24. Work with your attorney to create a subscription agreement listing the materials given to the potential investor.

25. Include a line that identifies the amount of the investment and what the investor is to receive in return.

26. Ensure that the subscription agreement includes wording to the effect that the investor has reviewed the materials and has had an opportunity to ask questions and review any other requested materials that you could reasonably provide to them. The subscription agreement affirms that the investors are aware of the risks of the investment.

27. Place a statement at the end by which the business accepts the subscription, then sign and date it in the capacity of your official position.

28. Make sure the investor manually signs and dates the subscription agreement and gives the document to you along with payment.

29. Make a photocopy of the fully executed subscription agreement and a copy of the investor's check for them to keep.

30. Take the check to the bank and deposit it in your business account.

31. Issue a certificate to each partner or member indicating your business name, the investor's name, the date of the issuance, and the type and amount of shares now owned by the investor.

DESIGN AND DEVELOP YOUR MARKETING STRATEGY PLAN

> Remember: "It takes marketing to cause the phone to ring."
> Joe Harless

1. Adopt a focus on individual customers' needs and how to drive opportunities.

2. Capture and clarify the client needs or pain points.

3. Make a strong diagnosis with the customer and provide a good prognosis and prescription for their pain.

4. Paint a clear and honest picture regarding how your products and services can help customers solve business problems.

5. Anticipate the organizational impact of the trends in technology and strategies for growing the business.

6. To generate leads and revenue, learn about how to produce content marketing to effectively communicate what you have to offer.

How to Get the Job

7. Learn to become an author and a publisher.

8. The subject matter experts and exemplary performers within your organization need to share their knowledge, experience, and time, contributing to content as well.

9. You can use things such as in-house created content, licensed content, videos, demos, and webinars.

10. Develop a social media strategy. Have key employees develop their personal brands so they can serve as ambassadors to your customer community and amplify your message.

> **Note: In God we trust, and everyone else must bring data.**

11. Use analytics and collaboration with employees to collect data and measure what you do with your marketing resources to increase the probability of a return on your marketing investment.

12. Produce a useful reporting process for everything you do that makes sense for your business.

13. Embrace technology such as Marketing Automation Pro and Web Analytics Guru.

14. Align internal talent that can stay focused on these skills.

DESIGN AND DEVELOP YOUR MANAGEMENT AND ORGANIZATION PLAN

1. If you need extra people support, determine if you are better off having employees or using independent contractors.

    - There are advantages and disadvantages to both options. This decision is critical because the legal and tax implications can be very complex. It is important that you seek advice from your professional support network regarding your specific situation.
    - This decision is also critical because the end result of your decision can affect the quality of your products and services and the reputation of your business.

If You Choose	Then
Employees	Ensure you create a written detailed legal employment agreement with the assistance of a qualified human resource expert/attorney. Include provisions for the following: • Job title and scope of duties • Terms of the employment agreement • Hours of employment • Paid employment expenses • Salary and benefits • Key person life insurance • Assignability • Confidentiality and noncompetition • Development and ownership of inventions, trade secrets, and new business ideas • Termination • The Fair Labor Standards Act • The Civil Rights Act of 1964 • Age Discrimination and Employment Act • Americans with Disabilities Act • The Occupational Safety and Health Act • Workers' compensation • The Employee Polygraph Protection Act of 1988 • The Electronic Communications Privacy Act of 1986 • The Family and Medical Leave Act • Employee benefits plans • Health insurance plans • Tax-qualified retirement plans • Section 401(k) plan • Supplemental compensation benefits • Equity-based benefits • Stock-purchase plans • Incentive stock option plan • Phantom stock and stock appreciation rights

Design and Develop Your Management and Organization Plan

If You Choose	Then
Contractors	Ensure you create and sign a written detailed legal agreement service contract with an attorney. The independent contractor assumes responsibility for their own taxes, health care premiums, workers' compensation, and unemployment insurance.

2. Identify the characteristics and skill attributes of new hires with high potential to succeed.

3. Create job profiles derived from exemplary performers. Use these profiles to make recommendations for enhancements to the employee-selection criteria and process.

4. Identify opportunities to ensure overall performance and shorten time to competence in the context of the work system. If you need more information, reference my web site: dougmead.com.

5. Identify what key marketing and sales employees are doing to be successful in their real-world contexts and identify how to promulgate these behaviors throughout your organization.

6. Identify how they produce results.

7. Identify how they obtain knowledge and continue to learn.

8. Identify what tools are most valuable to them.

9. Identify what creates barriers to their success.

10. Hire people who are smarter than you are.

11. Identify key management personnel and their qualifications.

How to Get the Job

12. Identify a compensation plan.

13. Identify the employee selection and hiring process.

14. Identify the potential use of outside professionals, including but not limited to the following:
    - Legal representation
    - Accounting representation
    - Consultants
    - Human resource professionals

DESIGN AND DEVELOP YOUR OPERATION PLAN

Describe the following:

- Geographic location

- Facilities, equipment, and layout

- Infrastructure

- Operating systems

- Hardware systems

- Software systems

- Accounting systems

- Bookkeeping resources, in-house and subcontracted

- Suppliers

- Work systems and all business processes

- Business performance criteria

- All employee job descriptions
- Ensure job descriptions include expected output and performance criteria for each position.

DESIGN AND DEVELOP YOUR IMPLEMENTATION PLAN

1. Clarify your implementation goals and standards.

2. Develop an action plan that will ensure your ethical business professionalism.

3. Search to see if a trademark is available for the name of your entity. A trademark is any word, phrase, slogan, design, or symbol that is used to distinguish a product or service.

4. Properly protect your trademark from being stolen, lost, or weakened.

5. To avoid having to change your trademark at a future date, perform a mark search prior to choosing a name for your business, product, or service and prior to filing to obtain federal trademark registration for the name of your company.
    - Performing the search can detect names used in all fifty states.
    - This critical research will also help you avoid future legal issues and rework because you chose a trademark that conflicts with another company's mark.

6. Seek advice from your network to identify other potential legal and/or operational problems and their likely causes.

7. Develop prevention plans.

8. Develop contingency plans.

DESIGN AND DEVELOP YOUR EXECUTIVE SUMMARY

Summarize the following data:

- Your business concept
- Your list of products and services
- Market segments and channels
- Estimate of market potential
- Starting capital required

DESIGN AND DEVELOP YOUR CONTINUOUS IMPROVEMENT PLAN TO SUSTAIN YOUR PROFESSIONAL PERFORMANCE OVER TIME

1. Whether you are working to get the job or starting your own business, learning how to demonstrate interpersonal skills is critical.
    - Continuous improvement means always searching for ways to get better at what you do.
    - If you are not growing, you are dying.
    - Seek out opportunities to continue to grow in your technical, managerial, and interpersonal skills.
    - Once you have the job, it is your interpersonal skills that will have a huge impact on your ability **to sustain** your job and career over time.
        - Interpersonal skills and your principles include the following, but are not limited to these:
            - Trust
            - Compassion
            - Integrity
            - Teamwork
            - Initiative
            - Nonverbal skills such as listening to others

- Honesty: the quality or state of being truthful, not deceptive
- Integrity: strict adherence to a standard of value or conduct; personal honesty and independence
- Respect for yourself and others
- Confidence: reliance or trust—a feeling of self-assurance
- Increased confidence in your abilities by being competent and positive and focusing on producing good output
- Responsibility: accounting for your actions
- Perseverance: to persist in an idea, purpose, or task despite obstacles
- To succeed you must continue through bad breaks and your own mistakes while learning from past experiences.
- Courtesy: considerate behavior toward others, including polite remarks or gestures
- Judgment: the ability to make a decision or form an opinion, or a decision reached after consideration. Making good choices and using good judgment are both very important in life. It comes into play when deciding on a strategy as well as when making healthy choices.

2. If you are starting your own company, it is your interpersonal skills and your principles that will make a significant difference in building and keeping your clients, customers, suppliers, and partnership base.

3. Study the results of your work. After getting this far in your strategic and tactical plan, you may think you have finally arrived.

4. Don't be fooled into thinking that you now have it made and that the process is over.

5. You need to continuously examine how well your plans are working and find ways to continuously improve your plan and your end results.

6. Reexamine your strategic and tactical plans often. These need to be living documents.

7. Review your progress.

8. Determine if your goals are taking you where you need to go.

9. Identify opportunities for improvement and learning.

10. Identify what you are doing to reduce vulnerability to control by something or someone else.

11. Determine if you need to add, delete, or change any goals, objectives, tasks and/or steps within the specifics of your plans.

12. Use your plans to guide your daily, weekly, and annual work direction to accomplish your vision.

13. Create a process that enables you to obtain feedback from your support network and your customers, and then study the results.
    a. Identify which process you will use to collect feedback data.
    b. Determine how you will obtain feedback and advice regarding how efficient and effective you are being in utilizing limited resources.
    c. Feedback will provide reinforcement for what is going well and information that will help you make adjustments to continuously improve your performance.

14. Document what you have learned as you go through each step in your planning process. For example, after each job interview or marketing opportunity with potential customers, sit down and develop revisions from what you have learned for improving each step in your work process.

Design and Develop Your Continuous Improvement Plan

15. Now is the time to reflect and realize that you have made it through some very tedious and difficult times. Now you have a chance to be happy again.

16. Look back at what you have learned and what you have accomplished.

17. Help others so that you can continue to grow and be happy.

18. Always focus on continuous improvement in your life and in the work processes that impact your life.

19. Finally, always remember to celebrate your success along the way with the people who have helped you achieve it.

ABOUT DOUG MEAD

Doug is a seasoned human performance consultant and practitioner, training developer, instructor, and personal business coach/mentor dedicated to helping clients design performance-based solutions that enable average performers to excel. Doug works with clients to find cost-effective ways to help people perform their jobs better. He also assists clients when they are creating entirely new jobs for new functions that didn't exist before.

Doug retired from Consumers Energy as a senior human performance consultant in March of 2012 after thirty-eight years of service. Doug is currently a principal consultant with Exemplary Performance, a human performance-improvement company based in Annapolis, Maryland. Doug brings over thirty years of experience directly supporting the utility industry. Doug also has extensive experience in the public and private sectors, often with Fortune 500 companies.

Doug completed his first human performance analysis over thirty years ago and has since completed work with clients on more than two hundred performance improvement projects. Doug is a human performance consultant/practitioner.

Doug's expertise lies in focusing on the following:
- Analysis and alignment to ensure teams and team members meet the same goals and objectives of the business
- Performance analysis to identify the key influences that enable exemplary performers to achieve outstanding results
- Design, development, testing, implementation, and evaluation of customized solutions for improving performance in critical job roles
- Assisting clients in implementing actions required to ensure successful, cost-effective, sustained performance and significant return on investment (ROI)
- Providing human performance training and coaching to people who have the responsibility to ensure exemplary human performance in their organization

Doug is a certified instructor of Joe Harless's Accomplishment Based Curriculum Development (ABCD) toolset, which includes certifications in front-end analysis, job aids workshops, and design and development workshops.

Doug is also certified to deliver the Expert OJT (On-The-Job) Training Workshop, better known as On-the-Job-Training.

Doug's purpose is to make a significant positive difference in the lives of others by helping individuals and organizations prosper and achieve their goals. He works side-by-side with clients to design and develop human performance programs that strengthen professional well-being, work systems, and performance results.

The most frequent use of performance technology is the diagnosis of problems of existing jobs.

Values: Doug values exceptional customer service and provides first-class customized service to meet or exceed client business needs and expectations.

Leading-edge expertise: Doug's specialty is in the analysis of human performance and the design of cost-effective interventions that support client business goals and strategies. His primary focus and experience area has been primarily in the energy industry.

Trust: Doug has experience you can trust, gained from partnerships with numerous clients on hundreds of successful performance improvement projects resulting in millions of dollars of return on investment, very satisfied customers, improved operating performance, and improved safety performance.

Doug is a long-standing member of the International Society for Performance Improvement (ISPI, www.ispi.org), and the American Society for Training and Development (ASTD, www.astd.org).

If you have questions, contact Doug through one of the options below.

e-mail: doug@dougmead.com

Website: www.dougmead.com

Blog: How to Achieve Peak Human Performance

www.ingramcontent.com/pod-product-compliance
Lightning Source LLC
Chambersburg PA
CBHW020904090426
42736CB00008B/497